CLIENT CONVERSATIONS

A Simulation and Video Learning Guide to Interviewing and Counseling

Jessica Rubin

Clinical Professor of Law and Director of Legal Practice
University of Connecticut School of Law

Jennifer Mailly

Clinical Professor of Law and Associate Dean for Experiential Education
University of Connecticut School of Law

WEST
ACADEMIC
PUBLISHING

© 2022 Jennifer Mailly, Jessica Rubin and LEG, Inc. d/b/a West Academic
    444 Cedar Street, Suite 700
    St. Paul, MN 55101
    1-877-888-1330

West, West Academic Publishing, and West Academic are trademarks of West Publishing Corporation, used under license.

Printed in the United States of America

ISBN: 978-1-63659-373-9

A NOTE FROM THE AUTHORS

We encourage teachers and students who use this video learning guide to contact us with questions, comments and suggestions for improvement at lawskillsvideos@uconn.edu.

JESSICA RUBIN
JENNIFER MAILLY

December 2021

TABLE OF CONTENTS

CLIENT CONVERSATIONS

A Simulation and Video Learning Guide to Interviewing and Counseling

CHAPTER 1

INTRODUCTION AND LEARNING OUTCOMES

HOW TO USE THIS LEARNING GUIDE

As Clinical Professors at the University of Connecticut School of Law, we created these videos to provide contemporary and discussion-provoking examples of lawyer-client conversations. The video materials consist of five client interviewing meetings and five counseling meetings, all showcasing lawyers employing varying styles and approaches to the same legal problem.

The legal problem is a will dispute between Jamie Hearn and Mic Snow. Hearn's mother, Eliza, recently died after being treated by Snow for an unrelated medical condition. Eliza Hearn bequeathed a controlling interest in the family business to Snow. Hearn believes that Snow took advantage of Eliza and seeks counsel to claim inheritance of the family business. Snow believes that the bequest is legitimate and reflects Eliza Hearn's appreciation for Snow's care and her desire to support Snow's healing practices.[1]

Throughout the interviewing and counseling meetings, the lawyers attempt to build rapport, gather facts, understand client goals, educate their clients about the law and assist their clients in making decisions. To adequately counsel their clients, the lawyers must explain the law concerning testamentary capacity and undue influence.

The lawyers in the videos demonstrate techniques along the spectrum of effectiveness, from good to bad to downright ugly. In some of the videos the lawyers were specifically instructed to demonstrate ineffective techniques. By showing both effective

---

[1] The lawyering scenario presented in these materials is a work of fiction and any resemblance to existing individuals or entities is unintentional.

1

and ineffective techniques, we aim to spark conversation, critique and commentary.

This Learning Guide provides a variety of ways for students to engage with the videos, whether in an in-person, flipped or remote classroom, in large- or small-group settings, on chats or discussion boards or as individual assignments. To assist instructors in incorporating these materials into their courses, we identify learning outcomes that may be achieved by use of the videos. This guide also contains simulation instructions, extensive discussion questions for each video and annotated transcripts highlighting the use and effect of lawyering approaches and techniques in each of the meetings. The materials also raise questions about the extent to which differences between the lawyer and client—including differences in race, ethnicity, gender and age—may impact rapport, information gathering and the development of a productive lawyer-client relationship.

Simulation Instructions: Simulations allow students to learn by participating in mock lawyering activities—as clients, lawyers and observers—and reflecting on the experiences of each exercise participant. We have included simulation instructions so that students may role-play and debrief the interviewing and counseling meetings depicted in the videos.[2] In addition to detailed role instructions for clients, lawyers and observers, this Learning Guide contains simulation preparation worksheets, debriefing questions and outlines for effective client interviewing and counseling meetings. Together, these materials guide students through the client interviewing and counseling processes, from planning to execution to reflection and critique. For optimal use of these materials, we recommend that students role-play the lawyer-client interactions before they view and critique the videos. This way, when students observe the recorded interviewing and counseling conversations, they bring a perspective gained from having participated in similar conversations themselves and have a basis for comparing and contrasting their experiences with the interactions set out in the videos.

---

[2]　The role instructions for each client will be provided by the instructor.

Discussion Questions: This Learning Guide contains discussion questions tailored to each video, with timestamps indicating where an instructor or student may pause the recording to consider questions, gauge reactions, offer commentary and evaluate the progress of the meeting. The discussion questions are designed to help students identify interviewing and counseling styles and techniques, and form opinions that will ultimately inform their own approaches to client representation.

Annotated Transcripts: As an additional or alternative vehicle for engaging with the videos, we have provided an annotated transcript of each interviewing and counseling conversation. The annotations pose questions about the use, purpose and effect of various lawyering techniques; suggest issues for reflection; and highlight comparisons and contrasts among the different lawyering approaches featured in the videos. The annotated transcripts offer opportunities for both group discussion and individual student work.

These client interviewing and counseling videos and learning guide are designed for use in clinical and field placement courses, as well as classes in lawyering skills, client representation, trial advocacy and professionalism. They are suited to supplement any legal skills textbook or serve as stand-alone lessons for use in experiential course orientations, negotiation programs or law office trainings. Whatever the course or context in which they are used, the videos and learning guide will help law students and legal professionals understand how choices about lawyering approaches and techniques affect the lawyer-client relationship and develop their own professional identity and style.

LEARNING OUTCOMES

The interviewing and counseling videos and learning guide are intended to teach students to assess varying approaches to client communication:

1. Beginning a Meeting

    a. Identify and evaluate the lawyer's use of icebreakers and rapport building efforts.

    b. Evaluate the adequacy and effectiveness of the lawyer's explanation of lawyer-client privilege.

    c. Evaluate how the lawyer's tone and conduct in the early moments of the meeting affects the tenor of the meeting.

    d. Identify and evaluate the lawyer's transition from opening a meeting to substantive interviewing/counseling.

2. Lawyer Nonverbal Conduct

    a. Identify and evaluate the effect of the lawyer's nonverbal conduct on gathering information and establishing rapport.

    b. Compare and contrast the lawyer's nonverbal conduct in each meeting and how it impacts the development of a lawyer-client relationship and the achievement of both participants' goals of the meeting.

3. Lawyer Tone/Attitude

    a. Identify and evaluate the lawyer's tone and attitude, e.g., empathetic, judgmental, arrogant or collaborative.

    b. Evaluate and explain how the lawyer's tone and attitude affects the client's demeanor, rapport development and information-gathering.

    c. Identify and evaluate how changes in a lawyer's tone affect the client and the lawyer-client relationship.

    d. Evaluate the lawyer's willingness to invite and respond to client questions.

4. Physical Setting

    a. Evaluate the extent to which the physical setting of the lawyer's office is conducive to establishing a lawyer-client relationship.

    b. Compare and contrast the physical settings of the meetings and how they affect the development of a lawyer-client relationship and the achievement of both participants' goals.

5. Client Attitude/Demeanor

    a. Identify when the client is open, honest and comfortable during the meetings.

    b. Identify and evaluate the techniques the lawyer uses to encourage and maintain client comfort and candor.

    c. Identify when the client is reluctant, rambling, hostile, dishonest, embarrassed or distraught.

    d. Identify and critique the techniques that the lawyer uses to address these challenges and the extent to which they are successful in facilitating communication.

Interviewing Learning Outcomes

1. Information Gathering

    a. Identify and evaluate the effectiveness of the lawyer's information gathering methods.

    b. Identify and evaluate the lawyer's use of the following questioning techniques:

        i. Open, closed and leading questions;

        ii. Drilling down from general topic to specifics (t-funneling);

        iii. Timeline questions;

        iv. Active listening and follow up; and

        v. Flexibility in response to client reactions and answers.

2. Client Goals

    a. Identify and evaluate whether and how the lawyer seeks to identify and understand client goals.

    b. Evaluate whether the lawyer understands the client's goals and whether the lawyer enlists the client's participation in confirmation of those goals.

    c. Evaluate whether the lawyer tailors the interview to those goals.

3. Next Steps

    a. Evaluate whether the lawyer adequately and explicitly explains the next steps in the legal process and the client's role in that process.

    b. Evaluate whether the lawyer's preliminary explanation of the law is clear, appropriate and properly identified as preliminary.

    c. Evaluate whether and how the lawyer clarifies the scope of the representation.

4. <u>Conclusion</u>

    a. Describe and evaluate other approaches and techniques the lawyer might use when interviewing the client and the impact of those choices.

    b. Identify and evaluate the extent to which similarities and differences between the lawyer and client affect communication and the development of a professional relationship.

    c. Identify and describe the ways in which the lawyer demonstrates a client-centered, collaborative or directive approach to interviewing.

Counseling Learning Outcomes

1. Explanation of the Law

    a. Evaluate whether the lawyer's explanation of the law is clear, relevant and tailored to the client's situation.

    b. Evaluate the lawyer's use of plain language when explaining the law.

    c. Evaluate whether the lawyer invites and answers the client's questions about the law and confirms the client's understanding of how the law impacts their situation.

2. Identification of Options

    a. Explain and evaluate whether and how the lawyer presents options to the client to address the legal situation.

    b. Evaluate whether the lawyer presents options that are clear, precise and appropriate.

    c. Explain and evaluate the extent to which the options presented are tailored to the client's goals.

    d. Evaluate the extent to which the lawyer enlists the client's participation in generating and evaluating options.

3. Decision-Making

    a. Identify how and evaluate the extent to which the lawyer involves the client in decision-making regarding options to address the client's legal situation and achieve the client's goals.

    b. Evaluate how and whether the lawyer adequately and explicitly explains the next steps in the process, including any deadlines and requirements the client must attend to.

    c. Evaluate the client's satisfaction with the decision-making process and the course of action selected, and how the lawyer's counsel and counseling style contributes to that satisfaction/dissatisfaction.

4. <u>Conclusion</u>

    a. Describe and evaluate other approaches and techniques the lawyer might choose when counseling the client and the impact of those choices.

    b. Identify and evaluate the extent to which similarities and differences between the lawyer and client affect communication and the development of a professional relationship.

    c. Identify and describe the ways in which the lawyer demonstrates a client-centered, collaborative or directive approach to counseling.

CHAPTER 2

SIMULATION MATERIALS FOR STUDENTS

LEARNING THROUGH SIMULATIONS

Lawyering simulations provide an opportunity to learn by doing. You can experiment with different lawyering strategies and techniques and see how they feel to you and to your client. The interviewing and counseling simulations that are contained in these materials present a structured opportunity to practice your developing lawyering skills while working to resolve a realistic legal problem. Whether you are assigned to role-play a lawyer, client or observer, the materials will guide you through the stages of preparation, performance, feedback and reflection.[3] After you do the simulations, you can watch and discuss the video recordings of experienced lawyers handling the same problem. These videos will provide you with additional examples of interviewing and counseling styles and techniques and facilitate further reflection on their use and impact.

GENERAL INSTRUCTIONS

In these interviewing and counseling simulations, you will meet in small groups to role-play or observe a lawyer-client meeting. Simulations may also be observed live by a faculty member or the entire class (in a "fishbowl setting"), or be recorded for review by the participants, faculty or other students. Optimally, one or two students will play the role of lawyers, one student will play the role of the client and one or two students will observe. While participating in the exercises,

---

[3] These simulation materials have been developed over twenty years of our teaching in the University of Connecticut School of Law's Legal Practice Program, which at its inception drew upon the pedagogy and materials of New York University School of Law's Lawyering Program. We gratefully acknowledge NYU's contributions to lawyering skills instruction, on which we built our Legal Practice Program and the simulation materials contained in this guide.

you should experiment with the strategies and techniques for effective client interviewing and counseling that you are learning in class. The simulated meetings and post-exercise discussions will help you think about a variety of issues, both substantive (what to discuss and how) and interpersonal (what kind of relationship to establish between the lawyer(s) and client, and how that relationship is achieved). Another important goal of these simulations is to guide you through a reflective process whereby you learn from your own in-role experiences and from sharing ideas and exchanging frank and constructive feedback with other students and faculty.

PREPARATION FOR THE EXERCISES

If you are a **Lawyer**, examine your role instructions and consider your objectives and the methods that you will employ to accomplish them. As you plan for your interviewing and counseling meetings, consult the meeting outlines (pages 14 and 19), the questions and issues raised in the interview and counseling planning worksheets (pages 16 and 21) and the interview and counseling debriefing/reflecting worksheets (pages 17 and 22) included in these materials. If you are paired with another student to jointly conduct the meeting, communicate with your partner to prepare your agenda and how you will collaborate during the meeting. Allocate responsibilities so that each lawyer has a significant role and is an active participant in the conversation. You need not do any outside research to prepare for the interviews, but you will need to do research before the counseling meetings.

If you are a **Client**, study your role instructions provided by the instructor and think about how the person you will play might behave and feel while consulting a lawyer. Your emotional tone is as important as the factual information you convey to the lawyer. Learn the facts well enough that you do not have to refer to the role instructions. If you are asked for information that is not provided in the instructions, you may invent facts so long as they mesh with the facts that you have been given. As you prepare for your role, consider the questions posed in the interview and counseling debriefing/reflecting worksheets (pages 17 and 22) included in these materials. In order to preserve the realism of the simulation, do not discuss your role with any other student before your assigned meeting.

If you are an **Observer**, your primary role is to facilitate the post-exercise discussion. To prepare for this role, read your role instructions, review the meeting outlines (pages 14 and 19) and consider the questions raised in the interview and counseling debriefing/reflecting worksheets (pages 17 and 22) included in these materials. Think about how you would conduct the meeting if you were the lawyer. That will give you some baseline expectations for the meeting. You should also give thought to how you will provide feedback and encourage the other meeting participants to share their impressions and reflections. One approach is to begin by asking the lawyers to critique their own performances in terms of how well they met their own objectives and what they perceived as their client's objectives. The client and any other observers—including faculty—may then add their thoughts. You should encourage all participants to comment on what went well or less well (and why), ask and answer questions about their experiences and raise issues for reflection.

MEETING OUTLINE—INTERVIEWING

1. Prepare for the interview

    a. Research the client

    b. Familiarize yourself with areas of law that are likely to arise

    c. Identify potentially relevant broad topics and specific information you will address

    d. Consider the identity of the client and whether the client is seeking your counsel in their individual or representative capacity

    e. Consider confidentiality and potential conflicts of interest

    f. Create a physical environment that is welcoming and conducive to communication

2. Develop and maintain rapport throughout the interview

    a. Use active listening techniques

    b. Use engaged and respectful body language and nonjudgmental facial expressions

    c. Take notes but prioritize listening

    d. Convey attention and empathy

    e. Use mirroring and silence strategically

    f. Follow the client's lead in conversation and flag items to revisit

    g. Anticipate and watch for barriers to communication and consider strategies for overcoming them

3. Open the interview

    a. Use ice-breaking techniques to put the client at ease

    b. Preview what will happen during the interview and the goals of the meeting

    c. Explain lawyer-client confidentiality

4. Engage in information gathering

    a. Ask the client open-ended questions to start and give them freedom to tell their story

    b. Follow up with narrower questions to elicit and clarify details

    c. Use time-line questioning where appropriate

    d. Establish all relevant facts and their sources

    e. Learn all parties' interests and positions

5. Identify the client's goals

    a. Begin to elicit the client's problems and goals

    b. Develop potential legal issues and theories

6. Close the interview

    a. Review information provided by the client and confirm the client's goals

    b. Collect or request documents and other evidence relevant to the matter

    c. Clarify if you are retained by the client and the scope of that representation

    d. Explain the fee structure

    e. Check for any emergencies or urgent situations

    f. Offer some preliminary strategy

    g. Invite client questions and be honest in answering them

    h. Make a concrete plan for next steps, action items, deadlines and necessary interim actions

INTERVIEW PLANNING WORKSHEET

1. What are your goals for this interview?

2. How will you prepare the physical setting for the interview?

3. How do you plan to develop and maintain rapport?

4. Who is the client (in what role is the client seeking advice)? What can you learn about the client before the meeting? How will you gather information related to conflicts of interest?

5. How will you open the interview?

6. How will you obtain information that you need to address the client's concerns? How will you organize your questions? What questioning techniques will you use?

7. How will you cover your agenda and record what you learn?

8. What do you think are the client's expectations about the interview?

9. What legal questions do you anticipate and how will you address them?

10. What non-legal concerns do you anticipate coming up during the interview?

11. How will you elicit the client's goals?

12. How will you discuss legal fees and confidentiality?

13. What schedule and tasks will you establish for follow-up?

INTERVIEW DEBRIEFING/
REFLECTING WORKSHEET

1. At the beginning of the interview, what use was made of ice breakers? How effective were they in facilitating communication?

2. What kinds of questions did the lawyer use? When did open questions work best and when were closed questions useful? What was the impact of the use of different kinds of questions on the gathering of information and establishment/maintenance of rapport?

3. Was the lawyer listening to the client's answers? Were follow-up questions responsive?

4. Did the lawyer engage in active listening techniques? Which ones? How did they make the client feel?

5. Did the lawyer establish rapport with the client? What were the indicators of that rapport? How did the lawyer establish or fail to establish rapport?

6. Was the lawyer responsive to the client's questions? Did the lawyer answer them directly? Did the lawyer say when more information was needed in order to answer?

7. How thorough was the lawyer's information gathering? Did the lawyer use timeline questioning? Did the lawyer probe for details after events or issues were described?

8. Did the lawyer identify what the client sees as the problem?

9. Did the lawyer solicit the client's input about how the client would like to solve the problem and about the client's goals of the representation?

10. How did the client and lawyer feel about the lawyer's explanation of the applicable law?

11. Did the lawyer describe the fee structure and other aspects of the lawyer-client relationship?

12. Is it clear what the lawyer will do—and what the client will be expected to do—after the interview? Is the client comfortable with the plan?

13. How did the client feel throughout the interview? Were there certain actions on the part of the lawyer that made the client comfortable/uncomfortable?

14. Who controlled the interview? How did the client/lawyers feel about the allocation of control?

15. What did the lawyer do when the lawyer did not know the answer to a question?

16. How does the lawyer feel about the pre-interview planning? Was there anything the lawyer could have planned for that they failed to consider? Did the client feel that the lawyer was well prepared?

17. Is there anything that the lawyer would have done differently? Is there anything that the client or observer would have done differently?

18. If more than one lawyer conducted the interview, how did the lawyers plan for the allocation of responsibility among themselves? Were there difficulties with collaboration?

MEETING OUTLINE—COUNSELING

1. Prepare for counseling

    a. Research and synthesize facts and law

    b. Understand the client's goals

    c. Plan information to get and to give, including predictions and rationales

    d. Generate options and lists of pros and cons of each

2. Begin the meeting in a way that facilitates communication and client engagement

    a. Ensure a comfortable and welcoming setting for the meeting

    b. Explain roles and provide an overview of the meeting and decision-making process

    c. Remind the client of the decision that needs to be made, that it is their decision and that you will help by explaining the choices and reviewing the pros and cons of each

3. Update the client's information and clarify goals

    a. Ask about any changes in the client's situation

    b. Review the client's goals and do not impose your goals

4. Explain the relevant law and how it impacts the client's situation

    a. Use practical, personal and applied explanations

    b. Explain law with the level of detail and sophistication that is appropriate for the client

    c. Avoid a lecture, encourage questions and frequently check for understanding

5. Generate alternative solutions to the client's problem

    a. Outline all of the solutions that you plan to discuss and consider creating a list or chart for the client to follow

    b. Present alternatives neutrally and in an engaging manner

    c.   Ask the client to keep an open mind as you review each option

    d.   Ask the client if they see any additional options

6.   Identify consequences of each option

    a.   Discuss the advantages, costs and risks of each alternative

    b.   Ask the client to identify consequences that they see flowing from each alternative

    c.   Be sure to consider non-legal consequences, such as economic costs and benefits, practical conveniences and inconveniences, the effects on personal and professional relationships and reputational impact

7.   Evaluate options

    a.   Review the pros and cons of each option, including probability of success and risk of loss

    b.   Invite the client's input on this assessment

    c.   Actively encourage the client to weigh in with open ended questions that encourage them to talk

    d.   Understand the client's risk tolerance

8.   Facilitate the client's decision and plan how to implement it

    a.   Ask the client to decide

    b.   Address any issues causing indecision

    c.   If needed, further explore options and their consequences

    d.   Be willing to provide your opinion and ensure that it corresponds to the client's goals and priorities

COUNSELING PLANNING WORKSHEET

As you plan to counsel, consider the following questions. You may cover any topics that you feel are relevant to your interaction with this client and achievement of their goals.

1. What are your overall goals for this meeting?

2. What do you think are the client's expectations about the meeting and its outcome?

3. How will you begin the meeting?

4. How will you obtain information that you need about the client's concerns?

5. How do you plan to explore the client's goals?

6. How do you plan to explain the law to the client?

7. How will you relate the law to the client's situation?

8. How do you plan to generate options available to the client?

9. How will you explore the pros and cons (legal and otherwise) of each option?

10. How will you solicit the client's participation in this process?

11. What legal questions do you anticipate and how will you address them?

12. What non-legal concerns do you anticipate coming up during the interview?

13. How do you plan to facilitate the client's decision-making?

14. Do you have a recommended course of action? Will you share it with the client?

15. What would you do if you were this client? What would you do if you were in this situation yourself?

16. How do you plan to end the meeting?

COUNSELING DEBRIEFING/ REFLECTING WORKSHEET

1. What did the lawyer think that the client expected from the meeting?

2. At the beginning, did the lawyer explain the purpose of the meeting and provide a plan or agenda for the meeting?

3. Did the lawyer check for new information and/or changes in the client's goals? Did the lawyer explore the client's goals?

4. Did the lawyer continue their rapport building techniques?

5. How did the lawyer explain the law to the client? Was it effective? Was it relevant and converted into practical application?

6. How did the client and lawyer feel about the explanation of the law?

7. Was the lawyer responsive to the client's questions?

8. Did the lawyer continue to gather relevant information from the client?

9. How did the lawyer generate options available to the client? Was the client's input solicited?

10. Did the lawyer explore the pros and cons of each option? Did the client participate in this process? Were non-legal factors considered?

11. Describe how the lawyer facilitated the client's decision-making. Did the lawyer recommend a course of action?

12. How did the client feel throughout the meeting?

13. What did the lawyer do when unable to answer a question?

14. How does the lawyer feel about the planning for the meeting?

15. Is there anything that the lawyer would have done differently? Is there anything that the client or observer would have done differently?

CHAPTER 3

VIDEO MATERIALS

LEARNING THROUGH OBSERVATION
AND REFLECTION

The video materials provided with this Learning Guide offer opportunities to observe and reflect on a variety of approaches to client interviewing and counseling. The ten videos depict lawyers trying, some more effectively than others, to develop rapport, gather relevant information, understand client goals, explain the applicable law, discuss options and assist their clients to make decisions. By watching the videos, you will learn to identify, compare and evaluate different lawyering styles and techniques. The discussion questions and annotated transcripts that accompany the videos are designed to spur insight, reflection and dialogue.

To maximize the educational value of the video materials, we recommend that you role-play the interviewing and counseling meetings before watching the videos. That way, your reactions to the videos are informed by your own experiences, and you can compare and contrast your meetings with those you observe. Reading through the thematic questions in this chapter will highlight issues to consider while observing the video meetings. While watching the videos, take detailed notes about what was said, how it was said, the clients' reactions and your reactions. This will enable you to support your comments and critiques by referring to specific words, exchanges and behaviors, rather than general impressions.

By carefully observing and using the discussion questions and annotated transcripts to reflect on the conversations portrayed in the videos, you will learn how different lawyering styles and techniques affect the lawyer-client relationship and begin the process of developing your own professional style.

THEMATIC QUESTIONS

These questions raise themes that are central to the lawyer-client relationship: questions about allocating authority between lawyer and client, creating and maintaining rapport, promoting candid communication, facilitating informed decision-making and lawyering across differences. As you watch the videos, consider how these themes are reflected in the interviewing and counseling conversations.

Interviewing

Focus: Client-Centeredness

1. What does it mean for a lawyer to be client-centered? What are the hallmarks of client-centered lawyering? What are the advantages and challenges of a client-centered approach to lawyering? How does this approach compare to other lawyering styles?

2. How does a lawyer demonstrate empathy, understanding and non-judgment, and what is the value of doing so?

3. When should the lawyer talk and when should the lawyer listen? What does it mean to truly listen to the client? What is the impact of active listening on the lawyer-client relationship? What are the cues—nonverbal and verbal— from a client that signal that the lawyer should start or stop talking?

Focus: Fact-Finding

1. What questioning approaches—both in terms of the type and order of questions—are most effective in eliciting the client's story, goals and relevant facts?

2. How do rapport building, empathy and active listening affect information-gathering during the initial client interview?

3. What techniques can a lawyer use to elicit information from a client who is unfocused, nervous, fearful, hostile or upset?

4. How does a lawyer investigate embarrassing, unfavorable or damaging information about the client or their case

without impairing rapport with the client and creating barriers to communication?

Counseling

Focus: Explaining the Law and Presenting Options

1. How does a lawyer explain the legal rules or principles relevant to the client's case so that the client understands and can rely on that understanding to inform their decision-making?

2. How does the lawyer explain the operation of legal rules or the application of legal rules to the client's situation when there is uncertainty about the state of the law and/or its application?

3. How does a lawyer present the client with options and invite the client's input into the evaluation of those options and generation of additional options?

Focus: Facilitating Client Decision-Making

1. How does a lawyer gauge whether a client understands the potential outcomes/consequences of each option?

2. How does a lawyer facilitate client decision-making among options?

3. How does a lawyer consider the client's own values, priorities, preferences and risk-tolerance when facilitating client decision-making?

4. What are the advantages and disadvantages of a lawyer sharing their preferences or recommendations with the client?

5. When, if ever, is it appropriate for a lawyer to present their client only one option—the lawyer's recommended option—with no alternatives?

Focus: Lawyering Across Differences

1. In what ways do differences (or similarities) in race, ethnicity, gender and age between the lawyer and client affect their communications, rapport-building, mutual understanding and the resulting professional relationship?

2. What actions can lawyers take to reduce the risk that their interactions with clients are not adversely affected by bias, stereotype, assumptions and/or cultural insensitivity?

If you are assigned or otherwise plan to role-play the interview of Jamie Hearn, do not read beyond this page until you have completed the simulation.

CHAPTER 4

HEARN INTERVIEW 1

You are about to watch a lawyer conduct an initial client interview of Jamie Hearn. As you observe the interview, note how the lawyer chooses to conduct the interview and the impact of those choices on the client. Consider alternative approaches and techniques the lawyer could have used, and how you would have conducted this interview had you been the lawyer. Also consider the extent to which differences between the lawyer and client—differences in race, ethnicity, gender and age—may impact the dynamics between the lawyer and client.

DISCUSSION QUESTIONS

The following discussion questions highlight specific issues raised in this meeting. The timestamps indicate moments when you may pause the video to consider the questions and gauge your reactions to the lawyer-client conversation.

0:15 *and entire video*: Describe the lawyer's tone and body language throughout the meeting. How does her tone contribute to the overall energy of the meeting and the client's demeanor? How would you describe the client's tone? How does it change over the course of the meeting?

0:30 *and entire video*: The lawyer repeatedly interrupts the client from answering a question to ask him another. How does this conduct affect the information-gathering process throughout the entire meeting? What impact does this conduct have on the development of rapport?

2:00: The client reveals that his mother passed away not long after a tragic car accident. How does the lawyer respond to this? What is the impact of that response on the client and the tone of the meeting?

3:10: The lawyer asks the client about bringing a medical malpractice suit and continues to discuss a possible suit even though the client is upset and asks her to stop. How does this exchange affect the lawyer-client relationship? Should the lawyer mention such a claim at all when the client does not raise it? Why or why not?

4:05: The lawyer becomes annoyed and defensive when the client expresses that he does not want to discuss a medical malpractice suit. What might the lawyer be concerned about? How might the lawyer handle this exchange so as not to upset the client further and undermine rapport?

5:47: Referring to the client's mother, the lawyer says, "She died? Just like that?" How might the lawyer respond more appropriately? Are there more empathetic ways to address or acknowledge a client's grief or loss?

6:42: What does the lawyer assume here or fail to clarify? What are the hazards of making assumptions about a client's story or goals?

8:38: How does the lawyer react when she learns that the client settled hostile workplace claims by employees? How does the lawyer's reaction affect the client's willingness to share details about the claims? Why does the lawyer press the client for this information when the client so clearly does not want to reveal it? How might the lawyer probe the client's harassment claim in a way that does not undermine the lawyer-client relationship? How might the age and gender differences between the lawyer and client create additional barriers to communication about this sensitive issue?

FOR FURTHER DISCUSSION

1.   When the client expresses that he does not want to discuss a medical malpractice suit, the lawyer reminds the client that she is "very busy" and has "made time" for the client. What is the effect of this exchange on the client? How might the lawyer have handled her frustration more skillfully?

2.   What is the client's tone and demeanor throughout the meeting? Does he contribute to (or instigate) the combative

nature of the meeting? How might a lawyer address a client's hostile, apprehensive or otherwise negative attitude at the outset of or during the conversation?

3. What questioning techniques does the lawyer use to gather information: Does she ask open-ended or close-ended questions, or use the t-funneling method? What is the effect of assuming what the client will say next?

4. Throughout the meeting, the lawyer and client often interrupt and speak over each other. When a lawyer notices that this is happening, especially repeatedly, what is an appropriate way to remedy the situation?

5. Imagine you are another lawyer in the office and overhear the tone or specific exchanges during this meeting. What would you do?

ANNOTATED TRANSCRIPT

This annotated transcript is designed to be read as you watch the corresponding video. The annotations pose questions about the use, purpose and effect of various lawyering techniques; suggest issues for reflection; and highlight comparisons and contrasts among the different lawyering approaches featured in the videos.

Lawyer: So, uh, Jamie? Jamie Hearn?

Hearn: Yes.

Lawyer: Yeah, nice to meet you. Jen Mailly.

Hearn: Nice to meet you, Ms. Mailly.

Lawyer: Um, let me see. I've got notes here someplace. . .um, I don't know where it is. What, uh, what brings you here?

 1.1 In these first moments, does the lawyer set the stage for the development of rapport, open communication and a productive lawyer-client relationship? Why or why not? How do the lawyer's opening comments and demeanor compare with the lawyer's conduct at the outset of Hearn Interview 2? How might the contrasting styles affect the progress of the interview and the lawyer-client relationship?

Hearn: I'm here to dispute a will that was recently put into place by my mother, who passed away two months ago. There was an original will put into place that gave me control of the company, inheritance of her 55 percent.

Lawyer: Okay, when, when was this original will executed?

Hearn: About a year and a half—

Lawyer: Is that the first will that you know your mother made?

Hearn: —two years ago. Yes.

Lawyer: Okay. So, her first will was executed just relatively recently?

Hearn: Yes.

Lawyer: Okay.

Hearn: That is correct.

Lawyer: Alright. And how do you know about this first will?

Hearn: Well, I was there helping her write it. Um, my mother was involved in a car accident, um, around that time.

Lawyer: So, your mother has a bad car accident. She—at what point does, does she execute a will?

Hearn: The doctors told me very quickly that there was about a fifty percent chance of her making it. So, I sat down with her immediately. We contacted her lawyer, I brought in my lawyer and we, we worked on setting up a will in case worst came to worst, which she understood.

Lawyer: Did your mother think she was dying at the time that she executed this first will?

Hearn: She was well aware of the fact that she wasn't going— that there wasn't a certainty she was going to make it out of this, that there was going to be a battle that she could very well lose.

Lawyer: Okay, and at this point she agrees to leave you the remainder of the business?

1.2 What questioning techniques is the lawyer using to ascertain the nature of the client's legal problem? What are the advantages and disadvantages of these techniques? What questioning techniques would be more effective in encouraging client communication? How does the lawyer's approach to questioning—and her interrupting and anticipating the client's answers—impact rapport and information-gathering?

Hearn: Yes, the fif—her remaining fifty-five percent and full ownership of the company. And that's how I thought it was up until her passing recently, um, when I—that, that's what brings me here. There is another will now.

Lawyer: And what does this new will say?

Hearn: This new will gives her fifty-five percent—it still splits the liquid assets among my brothers and me, but gives the fifty-five percent to this, this Dr. Snow, um, who—I'll, I'll get into it in a bit. I have to talk about what happens after the accident first, though, otherwise none of it's going to make sense. She was still the president and CEO, but I'm, I'm like the unofficial interim, if you will.

Lawyer: While she's in the hospital.

Hearn: That is correct.

Lawyer: Recovering.

Hearn: That is correct.

Lawyer: Okay.

Hearn: I discovered shortly after she came out of the hospital, which is about two and a half months later, that she, she developed an addiction to painkillers.

Lawyer: Were these painkillers prescribed to her by doctors at the hospital?

Hearn: Yes. And we pressured the doctors, we got her off of those but she still was able to come into contact with painkillers somehow. I, I don't know, I haven't looked into those details.

Lawyer: Well, have you considered bringing a malpractice case against the doctors?

Hearn: I, I had not, but if you don't mind I'd rather, I'd rather—that's, that's just that's gonna have to be another issue for another time. I, uh—what's, what's most important—

Lawyer: Well, there are statutes of limitations. I don't want you to sit on your rights here. If you believe that the doctors at the hospital where your mother was admitted had prescribed painkillers that caused her to become addicted, you might want to consider a malpractice lawsuit—

Hearn: How—

Lawyer: —because the payout could be astronomical for a woman of your mother's, you know, a business owner, a woman in the prime of her life to be cut down by opioid addiction because of negligent doctors. You know, this is, this is something I think you and your family should consider.

Hearn: Listen, I—we really don't have time to talk about this. I'm sorry, I'm under a lot of pressure right now and that's something that I—

Lawyer: Okay, well, I'm under pressure too. As I said, I got a big case going.

Hearn: Alright, but this is my—

Lawyer: I'm making some time for you, but you don't want to talk about medical malpractice, you want to leave money on the table, that's your decision. Let's talk about the will.

 1.3 The lawyer advises the client to consider potential legal claims of which the client may be unaware. Is it inappropriate for the lawyer to raise the issue of medical malpractice and the statutes of limitations that might require prompt action to preserve the claim? How might the lawyer provide this information in a way that is more responsive to the client's interests and priorities?

Hearn: Let's talk about the will. I was the acting president and CEO while she was put on leave so that she could recover from this. Now, I encouraged her to receive a more traditional treatment, to receive more traditional help with recovering from this addiction. She instead sought out this Dr. Snow, who I was talking about way at the beginning, before we got into medical malpractice.

Lawyer: Mm-hmm.

Hearn: This, this guy . . . he, he, he took my mother on board for his alternative healing. She spent six months getting this alternative therapy treatment, which involved—I did the research—uh, the, the technique involves him directing electromagnetic pulses, uh, to the frontal lobe of the brain. And then comes back six months later and hallelujah! She's cured. She doesn't need the painkillers anymore—

Lawyer: Do you, do you know that to be the case?

Hearn: Uh, she stopped taking the painkillers. And it was—

Lawyer: How do you know? I mean a lot of addicts will tell you they've stopped when they really haven't stopped.

Hearn: She stopped exhibiting the symptoms. She stopped exhibiting—

Lawyer: So, she seemed better? To you?

Hearn: Well, yes. I guess I—you're right, I can't say for certain, uh, if she stopped, but there was a noticeable change in her behavior.

Lawyer: Was she able to work?

 1.4 Is this an active listening response to the client's previous statement? The lawyer is probing the client's mother's testamentary capacity, an important factor in a will dispute. Compare and contrast the lawyer's approach here with the lawyer's exploration of the client's mother's mental state in Hearn Interview 2. What techniques does each lawyer employ and what is the impact on rapport and information gathering?

Hearn: She was trying to get back to work. I was still acting as the president and CEO. We were on good terms. . .and then she died.

Lawyer: She died? Just like that?

 1.5 What does the lawyer's response here communicate to the client? What is the risk of this response? How would you react to this turn in the client's story?

Hearn: Yes.

Lawyer: Accident? Or. . .

Hearn: She went to sleep and never woke up. The doctors did an autopsy—they, they determined that there was a large tumor in the frontal lobe of her brain.

Lawyer: Ah, so the same lobe that she was getting electroshock therapy into.

Hearn: Yeah, or—

Lawyer: I see where you're going with this.

Hearn: —electromagnetic input. I mean, not, not electroshock. I, I don't, I don't know, but—

Lawyer: But whatever they were doing, they were doing it to the same part of the brain that she ends up getting a tumor in.

1.6 Does the lawyer really "see where [Hearn is] going with this"? In what ways does the lawyer impede the client from communicating the facts and his concerns so that the lawyer can fairly assess the situation and provide advice?

Hearn: Yes.

Lawyer: Mm-hmm.

Hearn: Yeah, that's my first cause for concern. My second cause for concern is, I go to execute the original will that we had worked on, uh, when my mother was in the hospital and—

Lawyer: She left the money to Snow.

Hearn: She le—yes. So, I called Snow and, you know, predictably told him, "What the hell? This, this is unacceptable. Why did— why, why—"

Lawyer: You think he had a part in this?

Hearn: I know he had a part in this. The new will—I looked into it—it was created on legalzoom.com, which, I mean, I don't know. I see ads on TV for that and the whole thing smells fishy to me.

Lawyer: She got a will off the internet.

Hearn: She got a will off the internet. You know the only presiding witnesses were Dr. Snow and my mother's lawyer.

Lawyer: Wait, wait, wait. So, your mother's lawyer was involved in this as well?

Hearn: Yes.

Lawyer: This is the same lawyer that was involved in the first will?

Hearn: Yes. I, I know, um, that that, that that complicates things but—

Lawyer: Well, it does complicate things. Because it means that your mother was getting counsel—

Hearn: So, Dr. Snow—

Lawyer: —for both the original will and the second will.

Hearn: Dr. Snow counseled her into giving, into giving him money. When I, when I, when I called him, when I asked what was the deal with this new will, which, you know, no one else in my family knew about, he said that my mother had asked him, uh, about the, the state of the foundation. To which he responded, "the business needs all the money that it can get." Well, this guy completely neglected to mention to her that he has—that he is the son of a drug-manufacturing magnate.

Lawyer: So, this is Snow. He's a trust fund kid.

Hearn: This is Snow. Yeah, he's a trust fund kid. He, he, he's a billionaire.

Lawyer: So what you're saying is he didn't need your mother's money.

Hearn: He did not need my mother's money, but he was not clear about her with that at all. And, you know, the, the biggest thing in all of this is that she was a recovering addict who had just been in a car crash a year ago, and had a tumor in her brain.

Lawyer: Well, are there reasons that your mother would have left the business to someone other than you?

Hearn: I, I mean. . .there. . .

Lawyer: How did it run when you were overseeing the business?

Hearn: It ran perfectly well from a business point of view. There was one incident with a couple of disgruntled employees but, that was settled out very quickly. I mean that's the only thing I—

Lawyer: Wait, you had to settle something with disgruntled employees? What kind of, what kind of claim was made?

Hearn: Uh. . .well, there were some people who had brought up that I was creating a "hostile working environment."

Lawyer: Wait, you're talking about sexual harassment?

Hearn: What? No!

Lawyer: They—"hostile work environment"?

Hearn: Yes.

Lawyer: That was—you just used that term.

Hearn: Yes.

Lawyer: Well, what exactly was the allegation?

 1.7 The lawyer is exploring the possibility that the client's mother intended to disinherit him. The lawyer in Hearn Interview 2 asks similar questions, with a very different outcome. Compare and contrast the lawyers' approaches to inquiring about Hearn's mother's motives in not leaving him the family business. What approaches are more effective in encouraging the client to respond to these difficult, and potentially embarrassing, questions?

Hearn: Look, I'd rather not go into that right now, I'm sorry. If that can—to whatever extent that can wait, I, I feel like all you need to know is that there was a hostile working environment and that it was settled. Okay? It was just an accusation—

Lawyer: Okay, well, with all due respect, I know what I need to know. And what I need to know is how you were running the business at the time that your mother was incapacitated—

Hearn: And what I told you is that I'm running the business just fine! The business was running just fine. There was one—

Lawyer: Well, incurring liability is not "fine." Liability for which you had to pay a settlement out of the business does not sound like you're running it fine.

Hearn: Listen, I really don't need advice on how to run my own f****** company!

Lawyer: Well, I'm not giving you advice on how to run your company. What I'm doing is giving you an assessment of whether we're going to be able to prove that Dr. Snow overwhelmed your mother's will and got her to leave him her business, or whether she left the business to him because you couldn't manage it correctly. That's what I'm trying to ascertain here. I'm sorry that it's upsetting you, but I need to know the truth or we can't go forward. So tell me about these sexual harassment claims.

Hearn: No. I'm sorry, I'm not, I'm not going to have this discussion with you.

Lawyer: Well then, I don't know how we can go forward. I need to know what it is—what skeletons are hanging in your closet before I can agree to take on a case that claims that your mother left her estate to some stranger instead of you because he exerted undue influence over him, as opposed to she made a conscious decision to cut you out of her will because you bollixed up the running of the business when she had—when she was incapacitated. Is that a possible explanation for what's going on here?

1.8 The lawyer continues to press the client for information that might reveal weaknesses in the client's claim. What is the lawyer's obligation to ascertain such information? Compare this lawyer's approach to assessing vulnerabilities in the client's case to how the lawyers in Hearn Interview 2 and Snow Interview 2 probe their clients for information that may undermine their claims. See notes 2.4 and 4.6. What techniques are effective in overcoming a client's resistance to sharing information the client perceives to be sensitive, embarrassing or damaging?

Hearn: Um, sure, whatever. Listen, I'm sorry, I'm done with this. I'm going, I'm going to speak to another lawyer now. Thank you very much for your time—

Lawyer: Alright. That is, that's your choice.

Hearn: —but that's, that's the end of this conversation.

Lawyer: Alright, I think you're gonna hear the same thing from another lawyer.

Hearn: Well, I guess that I'll have to find out by myself.

Lawyer: Alright.

Hearn: Without you involved.

1.9 How do the lawyer's conduct and demeanor throughout the interview contribute to this outcome? Review some of the lawyer-client exchanges where the lawyer's behavior undermines the development of a lawyer-client relationship. If you were the lawyer, how would you approach these exchanges with an aim toward creating and maintaining a more productive lawyer-client relationship?

Lawyer: Have a good day.

Hearn: Thank you.

The End

CHAPTER 5

HEARN INTERVIEW 2

You are about to watch a lawyer conduct an initial client interview of Jamie Hearn. As you observe the interview, note how the lawyer chooses to conduct the interview and the impact of those choices on the client. Consider alternative approaches and techniques the lawyer could have used, and how you would have conducted this interview had you been the lawyer. Also consider the extent to which differences between the lawyer and client—differences in race, ethnicity, gender and age—may impact the dynamics between the lawyer and client.

DISCUSSION QUESTIONS

The following discussion questions highlight specific issues raised in this meeting. The timestamps indicate moments when you may pause the video to consider the questions and gauge your reactions to the lawyer-client conversation.

0:00 *until* 0:30: What techniques does the lawyer use to open the meeting and begin to develop rapport? Does the lawyer's use of an icebreaker about the weather seem natural or forced? Does the client's response to the icebreaker provide the lawyer with insight into the client's situation?

0:40 *until* 2:30: Here, the client has the space and time to share her story. What does the lawyer do to facilitate this openness from the client? Should the lawyer have the floor here instead? Why or why not?

1:22 *and again at* 15:40: How does the lawyer assess the client's goals?

3:15: What questioning technique does the lawyer use here? Is it effective? Why?

5:38 *until* 6:52: The lawyer expresses some skepticism about the client's claims. What are the advantages and disadvantages of the lawyer challenging the client on her view of the facts? What techniques does the lawyer use to question the client about potentially conflicting, incomplete or damaging information while maintaining rapport and encouraging client communication?

7:42: The lawyer explains the attorney-client privilege in the middle of the meeting, rather than at the beginning. How accurately does the lawyer describe the privilege? What is the lawyer's aim in explaining the privilege at this point in the interview? What are the benefits or drawbacks of explaining privilege in the middle of an initial client interview rather than at the beginning?

8:10: The lawyer says, "I want you to be free and comfortable" as she invites the client to be honest and open. Beyond this statement, what techniques does the lawyer employ to encourage and motivate the client to provide candid answers to questions seeking what may be painful/embarrassing/difficult information? How successful are the lawyer's efforts? What more might the lawyer do to provide a comfortable space for her client to share?

8:34: The lawyer continues to press the client to provide sensitive and embarrassing information. What does the client's tone and body language communicate about how she is feeling about the questioning? How does the lawyer acknowledge and respond to the client's change in demeanor? How effective is the lawyer's response in maintaining rapport and information-sharing despite the intrusive and upsetting nature of the questioning? What other approaches might a lawyer try when repeated attempts to get a client to share sensitive information are fruitless?

14:25: In what ways are the lawyer's next steps tailored to the client's goals? In what way is the client involved in the next steps?

FOR FURTHER DISCUSSION

1. What questioning techniques and approaches are effective in communicating with a client who is visibly distraught or embarrassed?

2. How and why does the lawyer explore the emotional side of the client's relationship with her mother? What can a lawyer do to help the client open up about a personal or emotional matter, without making the client feel uncomfortable? Are the lawyer's comments on the complexities in the relationship between mother and daughter—and references to her own relationship with her mother—an effective technique of building rapport and encouraging communication?

3. At the end of the meeting, the lawyer begins to discuss a retainer before she confirms that the client wants to retain her. Is discussing a retainer an effective way to determine whether a lawyer has been hired? In what other ways does a lawyer clearly establish whether the client has hired them?

4. The lawyer spent much of the meeting inquiring about the client's background and experiences, but did not ask questions about Dr. Snow, the Khoo Yaa Daa Foundation or Snow's work with the client's mother. What are the benefits and risks of this approach?

5. Describe the lawyer's nonverbal conduct throughout the meeting and its effect on the client, rapport development and information-sharing?

ANNOTATED TRANSCRIPT

This annotated transcript is designed to be read as you watch the corresponding video. The annotations pose questions about the use, purpose and effect of various lawyering techniques; suggest issues for reflection; and highlight comparisons and contrasts among the different lawyering approaches featured in the videos.

Lawyer: Good afternoon, Ms. Hearn.

Hearn: Hi.

Lawyer: Good to see you in person.

Hearn: Yes, good to see you too.

Lawyer: You told me a little bit about your situation over the phone, but it's nice to see you in person.

Hearn: Yes.

Lawyer: Are you weathering this weather okay?

Hearn: You know, as best as I can. It's a bit of a heat wave out but, um. . .doing pretty alright. How about yourself?

Lawyer: Oh, I don't know. I grew up in a hot climate so it doesn't really bother me that much. What about you? Did you grow up in a hot or cold climate?

Hearn: Oh, the Northeast, so we got a little taste of everything.

Lawyer: Alrighty then. Well if you're ready, I'm ready to hear a little bit about your situation. Why don't we get started by you just telling me a little bit about what brings you here.

2.1 In these first moments, how does the lawyer set the stage for the development of rapport, open communication and a productive lawyer-client relationship? Compare the lawyer's opening comments and demeanor with the lawyer's conduct at the outset of Hearn Interview 1? How might the contrasting styles affect the progress of the interview and the lawyer-client relationship?

Hearn: Okay, um, my mother, Eliza Hearn, she was the owner of Unbridaled Wedding Apparel, our family business she started in 1974 with my uncle, Allen. Upon her death, I tried to execute a will she made where she agreed to give me her shares of the company upon her death, and the liquid assets would be split amongst me and my siblings. And, uh, upon execution of the will, I found out that she had made another one.

Lawyer: And what is it you're looking for a lawyer to help you with?

Hearn: I'm looking to either prove how this second will is not valid, or to force this Khoo Yaa Daa to relinquish the 55 percent. Because I did some digging, and this Mr. Snow—Dr. Snow, he is a billionaire. This guy has a fortune of like $3.6 billion and he's taking my mom's company?! It makes no sense to me. So, I— what spurred me to come here, I called up Dr. Snow and I used some colorful language and I accused him and I said: "Hey, you took advantage of my mother. There's no way that she would have done this, you need to give this back. What happened?" And I assume he's throwing some BS at me, because this guy says that while my mother was in recovery she asked, what can she do to help the foundation? Do they need anything? And he says they need as much money as they can get. "As much money as they can get," to a sick woman! That's what he says?! And apparently she wanted to give it all away.

Lawyer: And what was your mom's—and I know you're not a doctor or a psychiatrist, I'm not asking you for a professional opinion—but what was your mom's mental state at the time you discovered this second will, at the time she died?

Hearn: Upon her death, since it was so sudden, um, we had assumed maybe it had to do something with withdrawal? Um, but we had an autopsy performed and they found a huge tumor.

Lawyer: Okay. Let's go back to a point in time, let's say leading up to her death. It was—you, you told me it was sudden. Tell me what her life was like, let's say in the month preceding her death.

Hearn: After having been treated by Dr. Snow she was three months clean, and during those, um I think she came back the last month of the three months, um, and she was taking frequent trips to Florida—

Lawyer: Before we go to Florida—

Hearn: Sorry.

Lawyer: —let's, let's focus on that three-month period that she was clean and she came back. What was she like during that period?

Hearn: I think she looked at life differently now. Honestly, I don't know what this—the principles of this Khoo Yaa Daa is.

Lawyer: Neither do I, nor would I speculate. But can we perhaps speculate that one might behave a little bit differently after they've engaged in some form of treatment, whether we agree with it or not? So, during that three-month period did you see anything that was alarming or concerning or that, you know, having to do with her mental—her thought process, that suggests that she was off in some way?

Hearn: The trouble is she was going to Florida every three weeks for, maybe, three days at a time for a long weekend. But then, after we threw her that party, she went to Florida for probably the longest time she went, which was a week and a half. And during that time she didn't talk to me much, and generally we try to talk at least once a day. But she—that whole week she didn't really talk to me. And the week prior to that. So I think that may have been the time. I think that, if she was in the right state of mind, I think if she was sober, she never would have done what she did.

Lawyer: Did she travel to and from alone?

Hearn: She did, actually. So I would drop her off at the airport for the most part.

Lawyer: Did she make her own reservations? And, you know, buy her own tickets and so forth?

2.2 What questioning techniques is the lawyer employing to elicit information about the time period after the client's mother returned from her treatment at Khoo Yaa Daa? What are the advantages and disadvantages of the lawyer's approach to questioning? How does the lawyer's sequencing of open and closed questions impact rapport and information gathering?

Hearn: We do have an assistant who helps with that, um, at our corporate office.

Lawyer: I guess I'm not—what I'm missing, Jamie, is the piece when she—you said, "if she was sober." Either I'm misunderstanding or I was of the impression that by the time that second will possibly came into play—and we can't say for sure—that your mom was sober. You, your suspicion is that it occurred during that week when she took the extended trip to Florida, and that was shortly after she had gotten clean, and you all had given her the big party.

Hearn: Mm-hmm.

Lawyer: She was going back and forth to Florida, but she went this time for the longest period of time. Is that right?

Hearn: That's correct.

Lawyer: So, you just said to me that, you think your mom would want you to bring the challenge "if she was sober." At what point are you suggesting that she wasn't sober? I mean, I know about the first addiction and all of that, but at what point during that—this possibly executing, on her part, the second will?

Hearn: What I'm suggesting is that the second time, after we threw her the party, I think her dependence on opioids was swapped out for a different kind of dependence. And I, personally, I think it has to do with this Mr.—Dr. Mark Snow. She hates Florida! She doesn't even like humidity! And all of a sudden she's going down every two weekends?

Lawyer: On her own. Making her own arrangements. Coming back, seemingly fine. Going again. So she's an adult, and let me just say this to you, everything we do here and say here is in the strictest of confidence.

Hearn: Mm-hmm.

Lawyer: We have now established what is referred to as an attorney-client privilege, so everything you say to me is privileged from this point forward. Meaning that I can't share that with anybody. The only obligation I would have to, to divulge something you tell me is if you told me something about harm you intended to do to yourself or to someone else. So I want you to be free and comfortable and sometimes when I press you on issues or challenge you on issues, it's not that I don't believe you, but it's because I'm anticipating what the challenge might be were we to bring this in court. So I'm thinking like the other lawyer might be thinking sometimes in our conversation. So, I wanted to say that because I am gonna just challenge you, push back just a little bit. Everything you've told me up to this point suggests to me that, yeah, you and your mom, like all moms and daughters, have their, you know, back and forth and every day is not rosy. I think a lot of moms and daughters have that clash because they see so much of themselves in each other—I know that's true for me and my daughter. But you described to me also a period of time where things were good between the two of you, or at least had gotten to a good place. You were working in the business together. She'd, you know, overcome her addiction, so to speak. So, I'm wondering if you could tell me your thoughts about why she would have written you out of the will.

Hearn: You know, I—everything was so, so busy in my eyes, things just kind of breezed by me, you know. I didn't really expect her to die when she did, I didn't really expect that at all. So, um, when she did, it—that's why I'm here, that's the huge shock, so I really—I think it was her healing, honestly. I think that's what drew her away from me, perhaps.

Lawyer: Perhaps, Jamie, but don't forget what I told you about our relationship—our privileged, confidential relationship—and recall what I just said a moment ago about it not being uncommon that mother and daughter have some clashes from time to time. But to take the extreme position of writing you totally out of the will . . .

2.3 The lawyer cites facts the client has shared to challenge the client's view that the second will was not the product of her mother's free will. What techniques does the lawyer use to maintain rapport with the client and encourage her to continue to share information, even as the lawyer probes for facts that may be sensitive and embarrassing, and that may undermine the client's claim? Why does the lawyer choose this opportunity to discuss the confidential nature of their communications?

Hearn: That's—that's the thing. I don't know how she thinks that this—you know I'm not—as much of a good daughter I was I'm not perfect. No one's—

Lawyer: That's, that's—I get that, but what are you—

Hearn: I had a suit filed against me, um, like nine months ago. I, uh—since my work is kind of my life, I—and life is my work, I, I misstepped. I misstepped. I, um, I was sued for, um, some workplace harassment.

Lawyer: Workplace harassment. . .

Hearn: It was, um, sexual harassment.

Lawyer: Sexual harassment. And you said this suit was brought by employees? One or more employees?

Hearn: Five.

Lawyer: Five employees. All five alleging sexual harassment?

Hearn: Yes.

Lawyer: Okay. And they named you as their harasser?

Hearn: Yes. Yes. I'm sorry, I went to some workshops for it but it's still a bane to bring up, honestly. But I know you have to know it, and. . .

Lawyer: I do have to know it. And I need to know just a little bit more about it, okay?

Hearn: Okay.

Lawyer: Alright, I know it's not easy to talk about. But it was five employees—are they still in your employ?

Hearn: They are, yes.

Lawyer: Male? Female employees? Both?

Hearn: Both.

Lawyer: So, tell me about the suit.

Hearn: It all started at, um, a Christmas party. I was, um, showing some kind of risqué photos on my phone to some employees, um, and asking maybe too many personal questions about their, um, sex life in—at the time I didn't realize about, um, as president of the company what kind of power dynamics I have with people, so I should have realized that. And it, it was kind of—it was repeated, honestly.

Lawyer: So it's five different individuals? All five brought individual claims against you for sexual harassment?

Hearn: Yes, that's true.

Lawyer: And did they name the business as a defendant?

Hearn: Yes, so I used the Unbridaled Wedding Apparel lawyer to assist me with this.

Lawyer: So how did it, how did it resolve?

Hearn: It resolved with a settlement of $25,000. So, five thousand to each individ—

Lawyer: Five thousand to each, not twenty-five thousand to each?

Hearn: Yes, five thousand to each.

Lawyer: And they're still in your employ. What's, what's the atmosphere like now?

Hearn: Out of the five, four of them and I are now on good terms. I have apologized to all of them with sincerity and assured them that I would never, um, do that again, and they did all seem to accept my apology.

2.4 The client discloses details about the sexual harassment claims brought against her by five employees and the terms of the settlement of those claims. What techniques does the lawyer use to encourage the client to share this information that is both personally embarrassing and potentially damaging to her undue influence claim? Compare the lawyer's reaction to the client's disclosure of the sexual harassment claims and her inquiries into the details with the lawyer's response to the same disclosure in Hearn Interview 1. See note 1.8.

Lawyer: Okay, then let's talk a little bit about next steps. I guess in the immediate, I'm going to have to just do a little bit of research and see if there are some viable challenges you could bring, if that's what you're certain you want to do.

Hearn: Mm-hmm, definitely.

Lawyer: So I probably would be asking you for an upfront retainer of no less than $5,000. Of course, if we don't need all of that then we'll reimburse you, but that would be a good place for us to start and for me to get going on the research. We know there's already a court hearing scheduled so I can already anticipate that that's two, three hours. The research, I think at a minimum, I could get it done in a couple of hours—

Hearn: Great.

Lawyer: —and then we'll take it from there. So, financially, how does this look for you?

2.5 How well does the lawyer explain the costs of representation? What additional information should the lawyer provide for the client to make an informed decision regarding the costs of retaining the lawyer to handle the will dispute?

Hearn: Financially, I can do it. I, I have some money saved up, um, for this retainer.

Lawyer: The thing that I wanted to hear from you when I asked you what it was you wanted to do, and you answered me in two or three different ways, but directly you said to me that you want to challenge the will. And having now had this discussion, is that what you want to do?

Hearn: Definitely.

Lawyer: Okay, so then that's what we'll do. And I'll be in touch.

Hearn: Thank you so much you.

Lawyer: Take care.

The End

If you are assigned or otherwise plan to role-play the interview of Mic Snow, do not read beyond this page until you have completed the simulation.

CHAPTER 6

SNOW INTERVIEW 1

You are about to watch a lawyer conduct an initial client interview of Mic Snow. As you observe the interview, note how the lawyer chooses to conduct the interview and the impact of those choices on the client. Consider alternative approaches and techniques the lawyer could have used, and how you would have conducted this interview had you been the lawyer. Also consider the extent to which differences between the lawyer and client—differences in race, ethnicity, gender and age—may impact the dynamics between the lawyer and client.

DISCUSSION QUESTIONS

The following discussion questions highlight specific issues raised in this meeting. The timestamps indicate moments when you may pause the video to consider the questions and gauge your reactions to the lawyer-client conversation.

1:27: The lawyer tells the client that "everything no matter what" is confidential. Is this an accurate explanation of the attorney-client privilege? What are the risks of describing the attorney-client privilege in this way?

1:33: The lawyer invites the client to tell her story by directing her to share "everything" she can remember about the situation. What are the advantages and disadvantages of beginning a client interview with a broad and open-ended question like this?

2:23: The lawyer says that the client has done "great work" and, throughout the video, makes other assumptions about the client's professional experience and success. How does this affect rapport and information-gathering? What are the risks of making assumptions like this?

7:47: The client expresses that she wants to avoid any legal conflict. Does the lawyer give the client conflicting information when discussing her options or leave out certain options that the client has? How? What might be the consequences of this?

What assumptions does the lawyer make about the client's goals, the mental state of Ms. Hearn, and the validity of the second will? What is the risk of the lawyer making these assumptions?

8:15: The lawyer says that he will "take care" of Ms. Hearn's son and that the client could "call him back and tell him that." Does the lawyer effectively communicate to the client what the lawyer will do to resolve the dispute? What are the risks of making such vague (and somewhat threatening) statements?

9:45: At this point in the lawyer's investigation, is it prudent for him to tell the client that she has a "terrific" shot at winning? How does a lawyer reassure a client that a matter can be resolved without over-promising a result?

FOR FURTHER DISCUSSION

1. If the lawyer feels prepared to give legal advice or present options before doing additional factual or legal research, should they do so during the initial client interview meeting? What are the risks and benefits of doing so?

2. What attitude is the lawyer conveying by his nonverbal conduct and tone throughout the meeting? How does the lawyer's attitude affect development of rapport between lawyer and client and information-gathering?

3. How does a lawyer inquire into matters that might reveal weaknesses or inconsistences in the client's legal position? What are the advantages and disadvantages of posing such questions at an initial client interview?

ANNOTATED TRANSCRIPT

This annotated transcript is designed to be read as you watch the corresponding video. The annotations pose questions about the use, purpose and effect of various lawyering techniques; suggest issues for reflection; and highlight comparisons and contrasts among the different lawyering approaches featured in the videos.

Lawyer: So, good morning Dr. Snow.

Snow: Hi there, how are you?

Lawyer: I'm well, how are you?

Snow: I'm okay. As best as can be in this situation.

Lawyer: Oh, something's wrong?

 3.1 How would you describe the tone and attitude the lawyer conveys in the opening moments of the interview? In what ways is the lawyer's verbal and non-verbal conduct likely to impede the development of rapport and information-gathering?

Snow: Yes, yeah. It's, um, I'm a healer and I've developed a technique that, um, helps people with their addiction issues. And recently I had a client who I was help, able to help cure and, in her gratitude, she, uh, left a bequest to my foundation. And then I got a phone call from one of her relatives who threatened me with legal action and, uh, sort of implied that there was some kind of impropriety. So, you know, I just wanted to talk with you today about those issues and see if you could give me some guidance.

Lawyer: Sure. Why, why did they imply there was some kind of impropriety?

Snow: Well, I think they thought that I had somehow, uh, influenced her to change her will, uh, to benefit my foundation. Um, I don't really think that's the case. I mean, I felt like her intention was to show gratitude for the work that I—we've been able to do for her, but I just, I just don't want to end up in a situation where, uh, I'm being accused of something.

Lawyer: Okay. Well, to start out with, I'll just tell you, you know, I'm glad you came in to talk to me about this. You know, everything that you tell me, no matter what, is confidential.

3.2 Does the lawyer correctly state the scope of the lawyer's duty of confidentiality? What are the risks of describing the duty in this way? How can a lawyer explain the duty of confidentiality with both brevity and accuracy?

Snow: Okay.

Lawyer: And I just want you to tell me everything you remember about this.

Snow: Okay. Um, alright. Where should I start?

Lawyer: Start at the very beginning.

Snow: Okay. Alright.

Lawyer: What, what was even the, the client's addiction issue?

3.3 When the client asks for guidance about how to tell her story, the lawyer tells her to "[s]tart at the very beginning." What are the advantages and disadvantages of this instruction? Is the lawyer's next question about the client's addiction consistent with his request to "tell me everything"? Why or why not?

Snow: The therapy that I've developed is, is sort of experimental. Novel.

Lawyer: Oh, I forgot to tell you, I have an appointment coming up in, like, another 20 minutes. So, I just need you to hurry it up a little bit.

Snow: Oh, oh, okay. Okay. Um, okay. So, um, her name was Eliza Hearn. She felt like her life had been completely turned around and, um, asked, uh, if it would be okay if she, um—you left some of her business to our foundation. Which I thought, that would be great. Um, and then she—

Lawyer: Right, cuz it sounds like you just did great work.

Snow: Yeah! Oh, yeah. Yeah.

Lawyer: So, you know, she wanted to give you money and, um, you basically were just trying to help her do that.

Snow: Yeah, that's, uh, that's a good, good synopsis. So, you know, she called me in and, uh, asked me to look over a will that she, um, had drawn up, uh, I think, and, um, I kind of helped her with that. We used one of those online will things and, um, and she had me sign it as a witness, uh, and then she left the bulk of her company, you know, to my foundation. Um, and then, you know, I was kind of surprised when she passed away, uh, shortly after that. Um, but I thought, okay, well, you know, her business really isn't one that I have any interest in running but I, you know, I do have a potential buyer lined up, so that would generate some income. And, uh, then I got this phone call, and I didn't really know what I—what to do about that. I really don't want to be embroiled in some kind of a lawsuit, I don't think I've done anything wrong, and I just need your help in sorting that out.

Lawyer: So, basically it sounds like, you know, you did some great work for her, she wants to give you something in her will, um, and now some lawyer is trying to tell you that that's not going to happen.

Snow: Well, it was her son that called me up and, and he kind of threatened me and, uh, uh, you know, threatened to take legal action and, and, and claimed that I'd somehow inappropriately influenced her to, uh, you know, to leave the company to my foundation. I think he's just mad that she chose not to leave it to him.

Lawyer: Is he getting anything in the will?

Snow: Uh, yeah, I think, uh, I think all the residual stuff goes to her family. I know the, you know, the bulk of her wealth is, is tied up in her business.

Lawyer: Do you know anything about how much money the business is worth?

Snow: Oh, uh, well, that's a good question. I'm not entirely sure how much it's worth but, um, probably, you know, a good chunk of change.

Lawyer: Okay. And you don't want to operate it, you said?

Snow: No, no, I—that's not, that's not my background at all. I have no interest in that.

Lawyer: Excuse me for one second. Um, so, uh, tell me about when you, uh, helped Ms. Hearn, did you say it was?

Snow: Yes. Yes.

Lawyer: Um, tell me about when you put the will together with her.

Snow: Oh, okay. Uh, so, when we put that together, um, we just, uh, uh, we used LegalZoom. We just found that online. We just did a Google search for, you know, "will forms," and, um, she had her lawyer present. He also signed that will. I'm not sure why, um, she didn't ask him to draft another will but, um, she thought this would just be simpler and I agreed, I encouraged her.

Lawyer: You didn't ask any questions about that?

Snow: Uh, no.

Lawyer: Okay.

Snow: Um, and, um, what it basically meant was that, um, uh, her shares in her company were going to devolve to my foundation to support the therapy that I've been using. Um, the foundation is called Khoo Yaa Daa, named after the type of therapy that we've developed. Uh, well, I don't know if you want to get into the specifics of the therapy or not, but—

Lawyer: Yeah, just quickly.

Snow: Sure. Um, so, so what it is, is it's sort of a novel approach using electromagnetic, um, pulses that are, uh, attached— sensors are attached to the frontal part of the skull and charges are sent directly to the brain, and this, uh, helps to curb impulses, helps with addiction issues.

Lawyer: Okay. And, um, you've gotten good results with that, with your clients?

Snow: Yes. Yes, so far.

Lawyer: Okay. Does that require any kind of a license or anything like that?

Snow: Um, it's experimental at the moment. We, we have not yet received FDA approval for this technique but, um, we hope to do so in future.

Lawyer: Okay. I just want to make sure you're not doing anything wrong.

3.4 Has the lawyer fully explored the nature of the client's healing practices? What techniques might the lawyer use to question the client about the quality, efficacy or regulatory authorization of the client's therapy?

Snow: I don't think so.

Lawyer: Okay. Alright, um, in terms of the conversation with the son, can you tell me, um, exactly what he told you?

Snow: Um, well, uh, you know, we had created this will using this online program. Um, I think she already had a will, and that was part of why he was upset about that. Um, you know, he felt like that was inappropriate, that it wasn't done legally but, I mean, we did use an online legal form, it seemed perfectly acceptable. Um, and I think his, uh, his problem was that he didn't end up getting the assets that he wanted, and so I'm not sure if his threats have any legal basis or not. That's really why I wanted to talk with you.

Lawyer: Okay. And so he basically just told you he was going to sue you?

Snow: Um, he threatened to try to take me to court about the will, which I don't want to do.

Lawyer: Yeah, so it sounds like he's, you know, totally out in left field, just inappropriate. Like, you've done everything you can to help his mother—

Snow: Oh. Oh, good. Okay.

Lawyer: —and, um, you know, she's really seen that value that your treatment has given her and, you know, the son is just trying to get money. Right?

Snow: That's, that's how I feel, yeah.

Lawyer: Yeah. Yeah. Okay, so, you know, I'm glad you came here. You know, we'll, we'll take care of the son. Don't worry about that.

Snow: Oh. Great!

Lawyer: You know, you can even call him back and tell him that.

Snow: Oh. Um, okay. I'm not sure I really want to have any more contact with him if I don't have to. I mean—

Lawyer: Okay. Well we can talk about that, then. You know, that'll, that'll be fine. Um, I may not have time to call him today—I'm busy—but we'll talk about the next steps on that one.

Snow: Okay. Well you've relieved, relieved me quite a bit.

Lawyer: The son is, is as I mentioned, you know, something that we can, we can take care of. That's inappropriate for him to call you, you know, don't—that, that's going to be something we can handle and, um, we'll get back to you on that. In terms of the will, um, you know, we will probably need a copy, you know, to see that, um, uh, going forward.

Snow: Okay.

Lawyer: I'm gonna need to do some work to assess, you know, um, sort of the legal context as to, um its, viability. But it sounds like, from your story, everything's fine and, you know, um, you have nothing to worry about, so.

Snow: Great, great.

Lawyer: Um, you know, we'll, uh, we'll make sure but, um, I like the—I, I sort of like the sound of your story quite a bit.

Snow: Okay, great. Yeah, I'd really like to get this resolved as quickly as possible because, you know, like I said, I don't really have a, a need for this business myself. I, I can't see running a wedding apparel business, but I definitely have a buyer lined up, uh, you know, if we can wrap this up as soon as possible. I think that would be in, you know, certainly in my best interests.

Lawyer: Just from what you've told me it sounds like a terrific shot at winning, so. Yeah, I'm not concerned.

3.5 Although this is the news the client wants to hear, does the lawyer have sufficient information to make this assurance to the client? What are the risks of over-promising a result? What more should the lawyer do to make an objective analysis of the client's legal situation?

Snow: Okay. I'd really like to avoid a lawsuit. Do you think we can, we can do that?

Lawyer: Yeah, there's always ways to try to avoid lawsuits. So, you know, you know, we can look at settling the case—

Snow: What does that mean?

Lawyer: It basically means you come to a compromise. So, you know, if, if you get something and the son gets something—

Snow: But, but why should you get something if the will is, is okay?

Lawyer: Well, to avoid a lawsuit, really. So if that's what your main goal is, then you know, then that is one way to achieve it.

Snow: Oh. So, to avoid a lawsuit I'd have to give up what should be mine?

Lawyer: Maybe. Some of it.

Snow: Really?

Lawyer: Mm-hmm. Yeah.

Snow: Hmm. Okay, I wasn't aware of that.

3.6 The client says repeatedly throughout the interview that she wants to avoid going to court and becoming involved in a lawsuit. Does the lawyer adequately explore the client's goals and priorities? What should the lawyer do to understand what the client is looking to achieve through the representation and why?

Lawyer: Yeah. Yeah, and this is all things we can talk about, um, you know, in the next meeting. So, um—

Snow: Okay.

Lawyer: —you know, if, if you come with a list of questions, we'll, we'll go through them and, um, and try to give you some more clarification.

Snow: Oh. Okay. And when will the next meeting be?

Lawyer: So, it's hard to know. Um, I have another thing to run to now, uh, but I should be able to get back to you by the end of the day with a time to set up the next meeting.

Snow: Okay. Alright. Okay, well, thank you. I appreciate your time.

Lawyer: Okay. Thank you very much for coming in.

Snow: Yeah.

Lawyer: Okay. Thanks.

The End

CHAPTER 7

SNOW INTERVIEW 2

You are about to watch a lawyer conduct an initial client interview of Mic Snow. As you observe the interview, note how the lawyer chooses to conduct the interview and the impact of those choices on the client. Consider alternative approaches and techniques the lawyer could have used, and how you would have conducted this interview had you been the lawyer. Also consider the extent to which differences between the lawyer and client—differences in race, ethnicity, gender and age—may impact the dynamics between the lawyer and client.

DISCUSSION QUESTIONS

The following discussion questions highlight specific issues raised in this meeting. The timestamps indicate moments when you may pause the video to consider the questions and gauge your reactions to the lawyer-client conversation.

0:24: Here, the lawyer begins the interview with an explanation of the attorney-client privilege. How accurate is this explanation? What are the advantages and disadvantages of explaining the privilege in the opening moments of an initial client interview?

1:30: What questioning techniques is the lawyer employing in the early stages of the interview? What are the risks and benefits of conducting the interview in this way? What is the impact of the use of these techniques on rapport development and information-gathering?

5:35: The lawyer asks whether the client was aware that the client's foundation was named in Ms. Hearn's will prior to her death. The client says that Ms. Hearn "took steps to make this happen." Do the lawyer's follow-up questions demonstrate active listening? If not, what would be an active listening response to the client's statement? What are the risks of failing to engage in active listening?

9:00 *to the end*: The lawyer says, "You're the decision-maker, the client drives the bus." Is this an effective analogy to the client's role in decision-making? Does the lawyer's statement comport with how she has been conducting the interview? What effect might this statement have on the client's understanding of the allocation of authority between his lawyer and himself?

9:14: The lawyer explains to the client that she may sometimes need to ask difficult or probing questions. Is her approach effective in motivating the client to share information? How? What other techniques could the lawyer use to encourage the client to answer probing questions openly and candidly?

12:45: The lawyer tells the client that he has two options: he can get more information about the probate estate himself or hire her to represent him in the probate process. What assumptions does the lawyer make about the client's goals? What assumptions does the lawyer make about the client's understanding of the law and legal processes? Is the client sufficiently informed about these options to make a decision?

13:30 *until* 13:52: The lawyer compares her role to that of a waiter in a fine restaurant; the lawyer presents the menu items and their corresponding costs, and the client chooses among them. Does this analogy accurately reflect the respective roles of the lawyer and client in deciding on a course of action? How does the "diner" analogy compare to the lawyer's earlier image of the client as "driving the bus"? How effectively does this image provide the client with insight into the financial and emotional costs of litigation?

FOR FURTHER DISCUSSION

1. How thorough is the lawyer's investigation of the client's foundation, its therapeutic techniques and the treatment of Ms. Hearn? The client mentions that his foundation engages in "experimental techniques" and that it has "cutting edge technology." Does the lawyer probe into the nature of those

techniques and how they might have affected the mental state of a patient such as Eliza Hearn? What are the risks of the lawyer failing to delve more deeply into these issues? How does a lawyer balance the need to maintain rapport with the client against the need to probe unfavorable facts? Does the lawyer here achieve that balance? How?

2. The lawyer does much of the talking throughout the meeting. Does the lawyer give the client sufficient space to tell his story and share his concerns? In what ways does the lawyer's tone and conduct inhibit client communication? How might the lawyer's use of active listening techniques allow for greater client participation in the meeting?

3. From 8:05–9:28, the lawyer explains that it is necessary for the client to give her the complete picture of what happened, including any damaging information that might negatively impact the client. Is this an effective means of motivating the client to share information that may undermine the client's claim or cast him in a negative light? Does the lawyer's tone facilitate or impede the client's willingness to share unfavorable facts?

4. The lawyer spends the first half of the meeting on information-gathering. She then reminds the client of the importance of full and candid disclosure. How might this reminder affect the client and the lawyer-client relationship?

5. Describe the lawyer's nonverbal conduct throughout the meeting and its effect on the client, rapport development and information-sharing?

ANNOTATED TRANSCRIPT

This annotated transcript is designed to be read as you watch the corresponding video. The annotations pose questions about the use, purpose and effect of various lawyering techniques; suggest issues for reflection; and highlight comparisons and contrasts among the different lawyering approaches featured in the videos.

Lawyer: Good morning Dr. Snow, I'm Regina Smith. How are you?

Snow: I'm good, how are you?

Lawyer: I'm fine, thank you.

Snow: Uh, Dr. Mic is fine.

Lawyer: Dr. Mic. Okay.

Snow: Yes.

Lawyer: So, you've talked to my office, you've made this appointment, we've done a conflicts check, and we're good to go. Anything you tell me in this interview is completely confidential, even though at this point we have not established a lawyer-client relationship—you haven't hired me—still, you're coming here with an expectation that everything you say is confidential. I understand, uh, only that this is something to do with a bequest in a will?

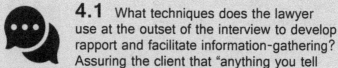

4.1 What techniques does the lawyer use at the outset of the interview to develop rapport and facilitate information-gathering? Assuring the client that "anything you tell me in this interview is completely confidential" may encourage the client to be more forthcoming in an interview and can operate as an ice-breaker. What are the risks of stating the duty of confidentiality in this way?

Snow: Yeah, that's right. So, um, Eliza, you know, god bless her soul.

Lawyer: Eliza what? What is her last name?

Snow: Eliza Hearn. Um, was somebody—

Lawyer: H-E-A-R-N.

Snow: A-R-N. Um, you know, was one of our, our success stories, you know, that ultimately had a kind of a tragic ending, which is unfortunate. We met her, uh, because she was having difficulties with opioids, and as part of my work I, I've come up with an experimental therapy to break the cycle of addiction. And we had great success with Eliza and she recognized that success in the work that we were doing. And so—

Lawyer: Well, let me interrupt for a minute. You say "we," are you part of a, a larger organization or a medical practice? Tell me a little bit about what organization you're working through.

Snow: It's the Khoo Yaa Daa Foundation.

Lawyer: Could you spell that for me, please?

Snow: I could, it's K-H-O-O-Y-A-A-D-A-A.

Lawyer: When did you establish this foundation?

Snow: This was established only a couple of years ago.

Lawyer: Are you the, uh, the director? What is your title with the foundation?

Snow: I am the director.

Lawyer: And what are your credentials? Are you a medical doctor? Ph.D.?

Snow: I do have a Ph.D. from, uh, Pacifica Graduate Institute.

Lawyer: What's your Ph.D. in?

Snow: Integrative healing and, um, therapeutic practices.

Lawyer: Alright. So, when did, uh, Ms. Hearn first come to see you?

Snow: Eliza must have come to see us at the foundation, you know, a little less than two years ago, I'd say shortly after we'd set up the foundation and were proceeding with our experimental techniques.

Lawyer: Let me ask, uh, is this an inpatient program?

Snow: She didn't have to live with us. We don't take people in, in terms of, I guess, what the foundation does, but there are a regular series of appointments. So, we saw her regularly over the course of a year.

Lawyer: Please define regularly for me.

Snow: Uh, this would be kind of bi-weekly. Sessions would last, you know, roughly an hour.

Lawyer: She treated with you for about a year, you said?

Snow: For about a year, yeah.

Lawyer: What happened, um, after that? Did she take a, a downturn? A relapse?

> **4.2** What questioning techniques does the lawyer use to elicit the client's story? What are the advantages and disadvantages of these techniques? How does the lawyer's approach to questioning impact the development of rapport, information-gathering and open communication between the lawyer and client? Are there questioning techniques that would be more effective at this early stage of the interview?

Snow: No, actually. Just tragically, Eliza passed away suddenly. It's very sad.

Lawyer: And when was that?

Snow: So that was, what, roughly six months ago?

Lawyer: Okay. Did she have other health problems?

Snow: None that I was aware of.

Lawyer: Do you know what her cause of death was?

Snow: I think they determined that there was some sort of brain tumor?

Lawyer: Okay. How, how did you come with—to that information?

Snow: Uh, that was information that, you know, the family was aware of and I, I guess I must have just heard from a secondhand source, so, I, I don't know, I didn't see the medical records myself.

Lawyer: Was there anything in her obituary about donations to a brain tumor foundation or anything like that, that would have given you a clue?

Snow: No, not that I saw there.

Lawyer: Alright. And when did you become aware that she had left a bequest in her will to the foundation?

Snow: That was brought to my attention, um, a couple months ago. After she passed, I guess. A couple months thereafter.

Lawyer: What bequest did she leave you in the will?

Snow: So, I mean, quite generously she decided to leave the, the shares of her company that she had—was previously the CEO of—to the foundation.

Lawyer: Okay. Have you seen an inventory for her estate?

 4.3 How would you evaluate this interview in terms of the lawyer's use of active listening techniques? How does active listening—or the lack thereof—affect rapport, client satisfaction and information-gathering? How well does the lawyer here balance her need for efficiency in eliciting the client's story and pinning down details against the client's need to tell his story in the way he chooses?

Snow: No. Not, not the entire estate, no.

Lawyer: Do you know how much those shares are valued?

Snow: I actually don't. I guess I just am aware that they would make for a sizable contribution to the work we do at the foundation.

Lawyer: Now, what problems have arisen since you were notified that there was a bequest in the will of this, these shares in the company?

Snow: I think the son is under the impression that the company would go to him.

Lawyer: Is he challenging the will?

Snow: Uh, I anticipate that that might be a, a problem in the future.

Lawyer: Well tell me a little bit about this company, uh, that is the subject of the bequest. Is this a publicly-traded company? Is it a closely held family business? What do you know about it?

Snow: It's a smaller, a smaller company. Clearly was originally designed as a, originally designed as a family-held company.

Lawyer: What's the name of the company?

Snow: Um, is it, wedding, uh, apparel. . .U-W-A. . .Unbridaled Wedding Apparel. I'm not, not into the wedding business myself.

Lawyer: Alright. Were you aware that you or your foundation had been named in Ms. Hearn's will prior to her death?

Snow: I did, yes. I mean, so, Eliza had taken steps to make this happen.

Lawyer: Well, when did you first become aware that she intended to include the foundation in her will?

Snow: Shockingly, near to when she passed. Prior to her passing, you know, she had approached me and, you know, made it clear that she wanted to contribute to the foundation.

 4.4 How might the lawyer use active listening techniques to respond to the client's statement that "[p]rior to her passing . . . [Eliza] had approached me and, you know, made it clear that she wanted to contribute to the foundation"? What areas of inquiry are suggested by the client's statement? Does the lawyer probe those issues? What are the risks of the lawyer's failure to actively listen?

Lawyer: Let me ask a couple questions about her, her, um, her thoughts and her actions at that time. Was she aware? You said she died suddenly, but was she aware that she was terminally ill or that, uh, she had a health problem when she made these changes? To your knowledge?

Snow: I don't think so. I think it was a, a shock to kind of everybody.

Lawyer: Okay. You indicated at the beginning that you had a very close relationship, a close personal relationship with her, and that you met with her after she had completed the treatment program.

Snow: Yeah.

Lawyer: What exactly was the nature of that relationship?

Snow: I mean, I tended to think of it as like a mentor-mentee kind of relationship.

Lawyer: And who was—who played which role? You indicated that she was older?

Snow: Yeah, interesting dynamic but, uh, she was just getting into kind of, kind of spiritual practices, right? So that, that's, I think, that was new to her, uh, after having come and visited us at the Khoo Yaa Daa Foundation. So, in that sense that's kind of how I was able to be a mentor to her. I think she was more open to kind of exploring some of those things after her experience with, um, the treatment that we gave her.

Lawyer: So, is it fair to say you had a spiritual relationship with her after her discharge?

 4.5 What type of active listening technique is the lawyer using in this exchange? What are the advantages and disadvantages of using this technique?

Snow: You know, I think that is fair. I hesitate to use that language a little bit. Like, clearly the foundation, the name itself, is based on Aramaic healing prayer, right? So there's a spiritual aspect, I think, to what we do, but the actual treatment that we've developed is, is wholly based upon Western scientific technique. Um, so I don't know, it's somewhere in between.

Lawyer: Let me talk a little bit about what my role might be to help you.

Snow: Okay, please do.

Lawyer: As a lawyer, I have a dual role. I'm an attorney and counselor at law. That means, part number one, if there is some sort of litigation, some sort of probate litigation based on whether or not you're entitled to take this bequest, my job is to advocate zealously for a client. But as a counselor at law, my job is not to tell you what you want to hear but what you need to hear, right? And I can only advise you if I know the good, the bad, and the ugly of your case.

Snow: Sure.

Lawyer: I need to know the worst thing that's going to be said about you, whether it's true or not, so I can prepare for it. I'm not here to judge you, I'm not here to judge, uh, anything that's happened in the past. I'm here to help you and to advocate for you and to give you advice. Now, you're free to take that advice or not take that advice—you're the decision-maker. The client drives the bus. But I can't give advice that you can rely on unless I know the whole story and all the facts. So, I'm gonna ask you some questions that may be uncomfortable, that may be a little bit probing, that may be blunt, but this is because I need to know, uh, what to expect. Because the worst thing that you can have is an attorney who's not prepared for some sort of allegation. The first time I hear something can't be when the other side brings it up.

4.6 As a preface to her turning to an investigation of possible weaknesses in the case, the lawyer explains to the client her role as an advocate and counselor, and that she needs to know "the good, the bad and the ugly" of the case to be fully prepared to represent the client's interests. In this an effective approach to motivating a client to share embarrassing, uncomfortable or harmful facts? Compare this lawyer's approach to probing "ugly" facts with how the lawyers in Hearn Interview 1 and Hearn Interview 2 seek to obtain information from Hearn about the hostile work environment claims. See notes 1.8 and 2.4. What distinguishes the effective approaches from the ineffective approaches?

Snow: I understand. Dealing with addicts, I understand exactly.

Lawyer: Okay. So, you indicated that your relationship with her was a mentor-mentee. I'm gonna ask you flat out, was there any intimate aspect of that relationship with her?

Snow: No.

Lawyer: Okay. Now, you said you weren't aware that she had an underlying medical issue, a brain tumor, or other issues besides being a recovering addict.

Snow: Right, yeah.

Lawyer: Did you notice any change in her personality or her, uh, mental acuity from the time that she finished treatment until the time she died?

Snow: Yeah, of course, but it all seemed to be related to her being free of opioids, right? When she first came in she clearly was a much different person. So, over the year that we spent together there were changes, but changes for the better.

Lawyer: Okay. So, no loss of memory? Loss of, of cognitive function? Analytic function? Anything negative that you noticed about her, her abilities in that respect?

Snow: Nothing. No, no, nothing.

Lawyer: Okay. Was she able to, uh, live independently at the time of her death?

Snow: Yeah, right until the very end. Sure.

Lawyer: She lived near the foundation, is that accurate?

Snow: Yes.

Lawyer: Had she lived near the foundation before her treatment?

Snow: That's how she found out about us in the first place. Like I said, this is cutting-edge technology, so just being physically close is actually what led her to find out about us and be able to get in on the ground level with the work that we were doing.

Lawyer: Have you or the foundation been sued?

Snow: No, we have not been sued.

Lawyer: Have there been any, uh, criminal investigations or accusations?

Snow: No.

Lawyer: Alright. In terms of your background, uh, is there anything in your background that Eliza's son might bring up to question your motives or your actions in this matter? Anything at all?

Snow: Um, I don't know. What kinda, what kinda stuff?

Lawyer: Have you ever been arrested?

Snow: I, I have.

Lawyer: For what?

Snow: For marijuana, once upon a time. But it's no big deal in this day and age, right?

Lawyer: For using? For selling? For manufacturing?

Snow: Personal, personal use.

Lawyer: Okay. Alright. How long ago was that?

Snow: Um, I mean, probably wouldn't have even been arrested in this, this era, but yeah, ten years ago.

Lawyer: Okay. I just want to know what's out there—

4.7 The lawyer is engaged in extensive fact-gathering by posing a series of closed questions. Is this an effective way to obtain the information she is seeking? What are the advantages and disadvantages of this approach? Compare the lawyer's fact-gathering in this interview with the lawyer's fact-gathering in Snow Interview 1. Which lawyer has a better understanding of the client's legal and factual situation? Why?

Snow: Yeah, I understand.

Lawyer: —before I find out from someone else. You weren't really clear about what objections Eliza's son had, except that, uh, he was unhappy and that this came as surprise to him. I understand you have concerns because a hint of a challenge has been raised.

Snow: That's right.

Lawyer: But at this point, there is no objection to the will, correct?

Snow: Not, not officially in any way that I know of.

Lawyer: Alright. So, at this point there's no action we can really take except to get more information about the probate estate. So, at this point, either you can do that yourself or you can hire my firm to represent you as a beneficiary in, in that probate process.

Snow: Okay.

Lawyer: And we can handle that for you. We need to value that asset—the executor should have been doing that already—we need to find out what the total inventory is, and we need to posture this case so that if a challenge comes that we can deal with it at that time.

Snow: Yeah, I'm not too worried about the costs. Money's not really an issue. It's not really what it's about for me, so. Yeah, that sounds good.

Lawyer: Well understand, as an attorney, I'd like to use an analogy that an older and wiser partner gave me once. Part of what I do is, is like a, a waiter at a fine restaurant, okay? You get the menu: on the left-hand side of the menu are all the choices that you have, everything from appetizers to dessert and after-dinner drinks. So, my job is to tell you what different steps we can take, whether it's depositions, hiring a private investigator, doing pretrial, uh, motion practice, all the different steps that can be taken that you can choose from, and my advice is to concentrate your efforts on maybe one or the other. In some cases, we need to go all out and do every single thing on that list. But on the right-hand side of any menu at a restaurant is the cost. And by cost, I'm not just talking about legal fees, right, dollars and cents. But what is the cost in terms of the emotional, uh, burden to you?

Snow: Sure.

Lawyer: What is the cost in terms of time? Because some of these things can be very time-consuming.

Snow: I value that as much as anything.

Lawyer: Okay. So, every step of the way my job is to tell you, this is what's possible for us to do right now, these are your choices, this is the service I can provide for you, but you're the one who decides what steps you want to take along the way. Is that a fair way to accomplish your goals?

 4.8 How does the lawyer's analogy to being a "waiter in a fine restaurant" comport with the principles of client-centered lawyering? Do you think that this is a helpful way to explain the roles of the lawyer and client and how decision-making authority is allocated between them?

Snow: That sounds good.

Lawyer: Okay. So, if you have any further questions, give me a call, we can talk over the phone. Let me know if you'd like us to send out an engagement letter to you. Obviously, call immediately if you get anything in the mail, uh, or by Marshal Service indicating that there has been a challenge to the will or to the bequest and we'll have to, uh, change tactics accordingly. Okay?

Snow: Sounds good.

Lawyer: Do you have any other questions right now?

Snow: No, it's just a lot of information. Um, no. I'll just process things as we kind of figure out that roadmap and get our menu together.

Lawyer: Okay, great. Alright. Alright, thanks. Great to meet you.

Snow: Nice meeting you as well.

Lawyer: Bye-bye.

Snow: Bye.

The End

CHAPTER 8

SNOW INTERVIEW 3

You are about to watch a lawyer conduct an initial client interview of Mic Snow. As you observe the interview, note how the lawyer chooses to conduct the interview and the impact of those choices on the client. Consider alternative approaches and techniques the lawyer could have used, and how you would have conducted this interview had you been the lawyer. Also consider the extent to which differences between the lawyer and client—differences in race, ethnicity, gender and age—may impact the dynamics between the lawyer and client.

DISCUSSION QUESTIONS

The following discussion questions highlight specific issues raised in this meeting. The timestamps indicate moments when you may pause the video to consider the questions and gauge your reactions to the lawyer-client conversation.

0:30 *and entire video*: Describe the lawyer's tone and attitude throughout the meeting. How does his tone contribute to the overall energy of the meeting and the client's demeanor? Consider the extent to which similarities in race, gender and age between the lawyer and client may explain the lawyer's attitude toward the client and the crude, profanity-laden manner in which he interacts with him. Might the lawyer's adoption of a certain older white male stereotype—crude, cursing, and sexist—be calculated to establish rapport with a client perceived to be of a similar background?

5:35: The lawyer is openly skeptical of the client's credentials, therapies and motivations toward his patients. The lawyer encourages the client to let his "hair down" and insinuates that the client is not telling the truth. What are the risks of this approach? What techniques could the lawyer use to assess the client's credibility without challenging him directly? Is the lawyer's explanation of the attorney-client privilege used effectively to motivate the client to be candid?

6:12: The client shares at least one goal in the video: he wants to know whether James Hearn "has a leg to stand on." How effectively does the lawyer address this question? Does the lawyer elicit any other goals from the client?

6:36: In trying to evaluate whether there was undue influence in the execution of the second will, the lawyer suggests to the client that it was the client's "idea" to execute the second will. Is this an effective way to get a complete and accurate understanding of the situation? When a lawyer suspects that a client is not being honest, or may be withholding damaging information about their case, what is an appropriate way to express this? How might the lawyer motivate the client to be more forthcoming? What might the client here say or do to allay the lawyer's doubts about the client's conduct and motivations?

8:52: The lawyer suggests that the client can use this case to send a message to others who may want to sue the client in the future. Is the lawyer identifying for the client a benefit of pursuing litigation or encouraging the client to use litigation as a threat and deterrent? What does the client's response indicate about how well the lawyer understands the client's goals?

FOR FURTHER DISCUSSION

1. In what ways does the lawyer's tone and behavior fail to meet the legal profession's standards of conduct and values? What effect may the lawyer's conduct have on the client's perception of lawyers and the legal profession?

2. Does the lawyer thoroughly investigate the facts surrounding Ms. Hearn's treatment and subsequent bequest to the foundation? What additional questions might the lawyer ask to obtain information and evidence relevant to the validity of the gift?

3. Does the lawyer make clear what the next steps are at the end of the meeting, and what the lawyer and client each will do to complete those steps?

4. What is the effect of the lawyer's nonverbal conduct throughout the meeting?

5. Imagine you are another lawyer in the same office and overhear the tone or specific exchanges during this meeting. What would you do?

ANNOTATED TRANSCRIPT

This annotated transcript is designed to be read as you watch the corresponding video. The annotations pose questions about the use, purpose and effect of various lawyering techniques; suggest issues for reflection; and highlight comparisons and contrasts among the different lawyering approaches featured in the videos.

Lawyer: How are ya?

Snow: Well, I'm okay. But I've got a problem.

Lawyer: Well, my name is Attorney DuBois, and my job is solving problems. So, before we get into the problem, I gotta ask you a couple of questions. Okay?

Snow: Go right ahead.

Lawyer: Alright, what's your name?

Snow: Dr. Mic Snow.

Lawyer: Like, I got a JD so you can call me a doctor.

Snow: Ph.D.

Lawyer: Oh, okay.

Snow: It's in integrative therapy and healing practices at Pacific University.

Lawyer: So where's that, like, California?

Snow: That's in California, yes, of course.

Lawyer: Okay. Do you work?

Snow: Yes.

Lawyer: Yeah, where do you work?

Snow: I'm the head of the Khoo Yaa Daa Foundation.

Lawyer: And what's your job?

Snow: I'm its creator and its founder. It's for treating opioid addiction and other kinds of addictions.

Lawyer: Oh. Alright.

5.1 The lawyer opens the interview with a series of closed questions seeking background information about the client and his profession. What are the advantages and disadvantages of beginning the interview this way? Compare this opening to the beginning of Snow Interviews 1 and 2. In what ways do the lawyers approach the initial questioning similarly and how do their approaches differ? How do their choices regarding questioning affect the development of rapport and fact-gathering?

Snow: You skeptical?

Lawyer: Well see, see, I have to ask you these questions for two reasons: one, for conflicts purposes.

Snow: Sure, go right ahead.

Lawyer: But the other, more important reason, for me, is to find out if you can pay my bill. So, so, you work for this foun—

Snow: There's no problem with paying your bill.

Lawyer: Okay. So, when did you set up this foundation?

Snow: About five years ago.

Lawyer: Okay. And it deals something with the opioids?

Snow: It does, it does. I discovered that proper application of strong electromagnetic impulses can actually affect inactive areas of the brain. And so, by stirring up this, um, this, this region of the brain—

Lawyer: Yeah.

Snow: —the need to have alcohol, uh, whatever it is that addicts you, whatever that—chiefly, it's opioid. Because that's where I've had my best successes.

Lawyer: So it works on everybody?

Snow: Well, I don't know that it works on everybody. I don't know believe it's a panacea.

Lawyer: Alright. So, you say "foundation," so what, what does that mean? So, like a 501(c)(3) nonprofit, or. . .

Snow: I fund it with some of the, uh, trust funds that I have and it goes directly into this foundation, and, and, and it, it pays for what I need to have done.

Lawyer: Yeah.

Snow: So, you know. . .

Lawyer: You charge people for this service?

Snow: They have asked if they can contribute. I will accept contributions. I'm not marketing, as I said.

Lawyer: Oh. So, like, I got an opioid problem, what do I do? Call you up, and. . .

Snow: Yeah! Yeah, I'd be happy to work with you. And see if it works, you know?

Lawyer: Yeah. And you do what? Put magnets on my head?

Snow: Well it's, that's—reduced to the most absurd terms, that's what happens. But there is a device with a strong electromagnet outside the, uh, the frontal lobe and, and, uh—

Lawyer: You put electricity in my head?

Snow: I'm not running any charges through anyone's head.

Lawyer: Yep.

Snow: It's just the presence of the electromagnetic field.

Lawyer: Well, alright. Alright. Well, you're not gonna cure me of my alcoholism.

 5.2 How would you characterize the lawyer's tone and attitude toward the client at the outset of—and throughout—the meeting? What does the lawyer's conduct and demeanor communicate to the client about the culture and values of the legal profession? As you watch the rest of this interview, consider the lawyer's conduct in terms of how it comports with client-centeredness and professionalism.

Snow: Well, you didn't ask me to do that.

Lawyer: So let's figure out why you're here.

Snow: Well, I came because I have a problem.

Lawyer: Oh yeah, what's that?

Snow: I got a guy who's calling me and threatening me. It's a fella named James, uh, Hearn. H-E-A-R-N.

Lawyer: Yep. H-E-R-N?

Snow: H-E-A-R-N.

Lawyer: H-E-A-R-N. James?

Snow: James.

Lawyer: Is that a lawyer?

Snow: No. Not as far as I know. He, um, he is the, I guess, he runs that bridal shop.

Lawyer: Okay, you lost me now.

Snow: Right, right, what's that got to do with anything? Well, it has to do with one of the people who came to me for treatments. And, uh, she was a woman who had an opioid addiction.

Lawyer: What was she taking? Oxycontin or something?

Snow: Everybody takes oxycontin. Anyway, um, so she wanted to know if she could help and, and she asked me about the foundation and, and I told her that, you know, I mean, it, it was a drain on the resources and if she, if she wanted to make a contribution that would be fine.

Lawyer: Oh, she wanted to help you?

Snow: That's what she said. I didn't ask her for it, she asked if I wanted her help. I said, "oh, sure." I mean, you know, I don't— didn't try to talk her into it, but—

Lawyer: What, she's gonna, like, put you in her will or something?

Snow: As a matter of fact, she did.

Lawyer: No s***?

Snow: No s***.

Lawyer: Wow.

Snow: She went to her lawyer and, and they came up with one of these LegalZoom things from the internet. I don't know if that's legal or not, I mean, that's not the way—

Lawyer: So the lawyer used LegalZoom?

Snow: That's what he did, yes.

Lawyer: S***.

Snow: Yeah. And, and he signed it and had me sign it and, and, uh, she put in the will that, that I should inherit the shares in her little bridal shop.

Lawyer: Yeah, what's it worth?

Snow: I have no idea what it's worth. The lady wanted to make me a gift and I didn't tell her no, you know. So, she did it and now the son is upset because he thought it was his company.

Lawyer: Yeah. Anybody else have any shares in this thing?

Snow: No, not to my knowledge. She was the sole stockholder, she was the CEO, and when she became addicted she stopped being CEO.

Lawyer: Why don't you just give it to him?

Snow: I could do that, yes. That's, that's one possibility.

Lawyer: You're rich, why do you care?

Snow: I don't see why I should back off from this.

 5.3 Refusing the bequest is an option that arguably should be considered. Does the lawyer effectively explore the client's interest in this option? How might the lawyer approach this option in a more client-centered manner?

Lawyer: You gotta understand here—anything we say together that's, like, confidential.

Snow: Sure. Sure.

Lawyer: Alright. So you can let your hair down, tell me the truth. I mean—

Snow: Truth? What do you mean by truth?

Lawyer: Well, you know. I mean, you got this little sch—thing going with your, uh, California degree and your helmet, and you got some rich broad gives you a f****** bridal shower, bridal store? It's a pretty good deal.

Snow: I don't know, it's—

Lawyer: How many of these have you gotten?

Snow: How many gifts?

Lawyer: Yeah!

Snow: This is the only one I know of.

Lawyer: Yeah? So far.

Snow: So far.

Lawyer: You got some other—

Snow: Well, I mean, if somebody wants to make me a present am I supposed to say no? I just want to know whether, whether this guy's got a leg to stand on. You know, I mean, he's claiming that I bilked him—you didn't ask, but the fact is that Mrs. Hearn has died.

Lawyer: Yeah, I kinda assumed that.

Snow: Well, you kinda—we're, we're talking about the will. She's gone, and, and so, you know, according to the will—

Lawyer: It's yours!

Snow: —the shares are mine.

Lawyer: Yeah. But this was kind of your idea, maybe?

Snow: No, it was not my idea, it was her idea. She came to me and asked me what she could do. You know, I didn't do anything I felt was unjustified. I mean, the woman comes to me and, and, and goes through the treatment plan, and—

Lawyer: Puts the magnets on her head. . .next thing you know, she's giving you money.

5.4 The lawyer is expressing skepticism about the client's therapy and motivations toward Ms. Hearn. What are the advantages and disadvantages of testing the client's credibility and probing weaknesses in the client's case? What strategies might the lawyer employ to test the client's view of the facts, inquire into sensitive matters, and raise possible counterarguments without undermining rapport and impairing the lawyer-client relationship? Compare the lawyers' strategies for probing "bad facts" in Hearn Interview 1, Hearn Interview 2 and Snow Interview 2. See notes 1.8, 2.4 and 4.6. Which strategies are most effective in motivating a client to share sensitive, embarrassing or damaging facts that might reveal weaknesses in the case?

Snow: I mean, there's no reason to behave that way. If it—if something works, you use it, right?

Lawyer: See, I think you're confusing coincidence with causation here. But that, that's legal terms—

Snow: Yeah, "legal terms," right. I, I didn't come in for a philosophical discussion, I want this guy taken care of!

Lawyer: So, okay. I call this guy up, he says, "go f*** yourself." What do we do next?

Snow: That's what I'm asking you. You're the lawyer, you tell me.

Lawyer: Yeah. Well, I mean—

Snow: I mean, you know, is he likely to sue me? What—he's, he's threatening suit. Does he have a case?

Lawyer: Well, has this will gone to probate?

Snow: Yes. Yeah.

Lawyer: Alright. So, what's, what's the—do you have a lawyer for that probate thing?

Snow: No. No.

Lawyer: So I could do that too?

Snow: You can do that.

Lawyer: Okay. Have you had a hearing over there yet or anything? Or is he—

Snow: No, he's just, he's just read the will and he's—you know.

Lawyer: Okay. So, will's been submitted—

Snow: The will's been submitted, he's like—

Lawyer: —and he's like, "s***."

Snow: "oh crap, the s***'s hit the fan," you know, kinda stuff. And he's calling me up as if it was something I did.

Lawyer: Yeah. Alright. So we, uh, call him up, he says, "go screw yourself," then I gotta figure out what to do, huh?

Snow: Basically, yes. Yeah.

Lawyer: Yeah, alright. Um, what else can I answer for you?

Snow: Well, meaning—what kind of exposure do I have in this thing?

Lawyer: Well, I suppose, you win, you get the bridal store.

Snow: Yeah.

Lawyer: You lose, he gets the bridal store.

Snow: Right.

Lawyer: There's a transactional cost—that's me and his lawyer, right?

Snow: Yeah.

Lawyer: So, you guys gotta figure it out. Is this a gold mine or a shaft? Is this worth fighting for? Yeah?

Snow: Well, yeah. Yeah. I mean, you know, up to a point everything has a price.

Lawyer: Well, yeah. But you're a man of independent means and wealth, so maybe you don't care. Right?

Snow: I—that's an option, yeah.

Lawyer: Well, I mean, you know, if—

Snow: But if I give him the shares, um—

Lawyer: Well, well, what I mean is, you bust his balls because the next time somebody gives you a car or a house or a store, you want them to know you're gonna go hell-bent for leather. The attack dog's gonna be on their ankle, and, and so they better not screw around with you.

Snow: What, what kind of a person do you think I am?

Lawyer: Well, I think you may be in this, kind of, for the money!

Snow: I categorically deny that. I'm—you know, this is, this is something that, it was her decision. Should I just give it to him and say—and go away and say forget it?

Lawyer: Yeah, well. I'll defend you to the full extent of your assets, is what I used to say.

Snow: Hahaha, right. Yeah.

Lawyer: Yeah. So, you want me to take a shot at this?

 5.5 How effectively does the lawyer counsel the client about the costs and benefits of litigating the bequest? As you review the discussion about the client's options, consider the ways in which it does and does not demonstrate client-centeredness. What does the lawyer communicate to the client about the client's decision-making authority?

Snow: I want you to see what you can do with it, yeah.

Lawyer: Yeah, yeah, and then I'll give you a call and tell you what's going on.

Snow: Yeah. Yeah.

Lawyer: Alright. Okay. Anything else you need?

Snow: Not at the present, no.

Lawyer: Okay. Alright. Well, my girl'll send you a, what's called a retainer.

Snow: A retainer.

Lawyer: Yeah. It's how much money I want to spend my time making these calls. And then, uh, I'll see what I can do.

 5.6 Does the lawyer adequately discuss the issue of legal fees before ending the interview? Do the lawyer and client have a clear understanding of the actions the lawyer will be taking on the client's behalf?

Snow: Okay. Thank you.

Lawyer: Alright. Good to meet ya.

Snow: Nice to meet you.

 5.7 Really? Throughout this interview the lawyer uses profanity, expresses skepticism about the client's honesty and motivations, and takes an exceedingly casual approach to the practice of law. Arguably, the lawyer's conduct in Hearn Interview 1 is not as egregious, yet that interview ends with the client angrily storming out. See note 1.9. What might explain the different outcome here? Consider whether the similarities in age, race and gender between the lawyer and client contribute to the rapport they seem to enjoy despite the lawyer's inadequacies in the rapport-building process. If you were interning for the lawyer and were present at this interview, how would you feel about what you had witnessed?

The End

If you are assigned or otherwise plan to role-play the counseling of Jamie Hearn, do not read beyond this page until you have completed the simulation.

CHAPTER 9

HEARN COUNSELING 1

You are about to watch a lawyer conduct a counseling meeting with client Jamie Hearn. Hearn has already met with the lawyer for an initial interview and is now returning to the lawyer's office to discuss legal options and decide on a course of action. As you observe the counseling meeting, note how the lawyer chooses to conduct the meeting and the impact of those choices on the client. Consider alternative approaches and techniques the lawyer could have used, and how you would have conducted this counseling meeting had you been the lawyer. Also consider the extent to which differences between the lawyer and client—differences in race, ethnicity, gender and age—may impact the dynamics between the lawyer and client.

DISCUSSION QUESTIONS

The following discussion questions highlight specific issues raised in this meeting. The timestamps indicate moments when you may pause the video to consider the questions and gauge your reactions to the lawyer-client conversation.

1:08: How effective are the lawyer's opening words in establishing rapport and setting a tone for the meeting? Are there better ways for the lawyer to address the fact that her previous meeting with the client had not ended well? Is the physical setting of the meeting conducive to lawyer-client communication?

What is the client's demeanor at the outset of the meeting? Is the lawyer's tone and attitude an effective response to the client's mood? Why or why not? How might the lawyer address the client's apparent dissatisfaction with the representation?

3:58: How clear is the lawyer's explanation of the law? Has the lawyer conveyed the relevant legal standards and how they apply to the client's situation? How should the lawyer respond to the client's requests for further clarification of the law?

Does the lawyer seem fully prepared for this counseling session? What is the significance of the fact that an associate prepared the research memo the lawyer is reading from? Should the lawyer explain to the client how, when and why legal work is delegated to others?

What does the lawyer's request that the client "let me do my lawyer thing" communicate to the client about her role in decision-making? In what other ways does the lawyer discount the client's input and opinions?

5:46: The client asks the lawyer for a list of options and the pros and cons of each option so that the client can review it and make a decision. Is this an unreasonable request? What are the advantages and disadvantages of giving a client a written list of options? Why might the lawyer here be resisting the client's request?

What is the effect of the lawyer stating that the client is "much younger" and labeling the client a "digital native"? How does the lawyer respond to the client's visible distress over how she is being treated? Does the lawyer's repetition to the client to "so don't worry about the judge" reassure the client? Why or why not? What steps could the lawyer take to ease the tension in the conversation and allay the client's concerns about the representation?

7:07: When the client mentions that the lawyer had been concerned at their initial meeting about her having settled workplace harassment claims, the lawyer states that she remembers their conversation differently and she has no such concern. What would be a more empathetic response?

The client asks, "So what's my role in this?" The lawyer responds, "You're my client." What does this response—and the way the lawyer treats the client throughout the interview—reveal about the lawyer's perception of the lawyer-client relationship?

FOR FURTHER DISCUSSION

1. How do the lawyer and client's attitude and body language affect the overall tone of the meeting? What could the lawyer do differently to improve the tone of the meeting?

2. Is the client correct to raise ethical concerns regarding the lawyer's plans to discuss her legal case while playing mahjongg with the judge? Why or why not? How does the implication that the lawyer can solve the issue through backchannels with the judge reflect on the legal profession?

3. What is your impression of the client's knowledge about the subject and her capacity to meaningfully participate in option assessment and decision-making? How could the lawyer more appropriately involve the client in the conversation?

4. What is the effect of the lawyer's instruction to "don't worry about it" in response to many of the client's concerns? How could the lawyer allay the client's concerns in a more effective manner?

5. Should a lawyer come up with different options for a client even if one option seems to the lawyer to be the best way to proceed? What are the risks of failing to consider or present other possibilities?

6. How might the differences in race and age between the lawyer and client affect their interaction? Do the lawyer's references to digital nativism and mah-jongg, and her assumption that the client works late hours reflect implicit biases and racialized stereotypes? The client is an accomplished business owner, yet the lawyer treats her as incapable of understanding and contributing to her legal case. What biases might be motivating the lawyer's dismissive attitude toward her client?

7. At the end of the meeting, are the next steps clear? Does the client fully understand what she is expected to do at the upcoming court hearing? Is she likely to be prepared for that appearance?

8. In what ways does the lawyer demonstrate directive, client-
    centered or collaborative approaches to client counseling?

ANNOTATED TRANSCRIPT

This annotated transcript is designed to be read as you watch the corresponding video. The annotations pose questions about the use, purpose and effect of various lawyering techniques; suggest issues for reflection; and highlight comparisons and contrasts among the different lawyering approaches featured in the videos.

Lawyer: Hey!

Hearn: Hi!

Lawyer: Hey, it's good to see you. I kind of had some, um, I didn't end the way we wanted to end. I'm really glad we are, you're here. And I, I'm really—um, I've spent a lot of time with your problem and I kind of know how we're gonna go.

Hearn: Okay.

Lawyer: I'm really, really excited about it cuz I think it's a really great way to go. It's kinda the only way.

 6.1 The lawyer acknowledges that the initial client meeting did not end well. Does the lawyer's effusive greeting and promise of a "solution" allay the client's concerns? What does the client's body language communicate about her state of mind? How might the lawyer address the client's negative emotions more effectively? Compare the lawyer's rapport building efforts at the beginning of this meeting with those of the lawyer in Hearn Counseling 2. See note 7.1. In the early moments of the meetings, what does each lawyer communicate about the client's role in making decisions about how the legal matter will be handled?

Hearn: Did you dis—like, look into my proposed ideas about how we can address this issue?

Lawyer: Oh yeah, yeah, yeah. I thought about all that. But I, I just—you just have to trust me, this is going to get you the result you want.

Hearn: Okay, so just tell me about it.

Lawyer: Um, so basically you had a lot of issues with Dr. Snow, I get it. This envelops everything. It gets you what you want, which is to get Dr. Snow, you know.

6.2 The lawyer brushes off the client's ideas about resolving the issue with Snow and asks the client to "trust" her. How does this approach comport with principles of collaborative or client-centered counseling? What is the lawyer communicating to the client about her role in decision-making? What are the risks of not inviting the client's input into the assessment of options?

Hearn: Okay, so just explain this technique.

Lawyer: And so, um, so, so we're gonna go attack. This is what we're gonna do. I like to use the word "we" because it's like we are doing it together, right? I'm a facilitator.

6.3 How does the lawyer's characterization of her role as a "facilitator" square with how she has conducted the meeting so far? What does the lawyer purport to be facilitating?

Hearn: Well, I just want to hear what your theory is.

Lawyer: So, um, okay, so pretty much, um, we're gonna prove by, uh, pursuant to Berkowitz versus Berkowitz, which is 147 Conn. 474, 42, 76, 77, we're gonna show that, um, we're gonna disprove the way that Dr. Snow—you believe—exerted undue influence on your mother and that ended up with will number two. So, so we're gonna go with the undue influence, um, theory, and there is this "burden shifting," but I think—I think I understand now from what the—my associate wrote in her legal memo that actually we're in an even better position because it's actually his job, his burden if you will, to prove that, um, to prove that he, uh, is entitled to that, that bounty so to speak. But that's again legalese and—that's his job, and then we can, then the burden shifts and we say nope.

 6.4 How does the lawyer's explanation of the law reflect her level of preparation for the counseling meeting? What is a lawyer's obligation when delegating legal work to others? Does the lawyer's reliance on an associate's memo raise ethical concerns?

Hearn: You're saying that Dr. Snow has the burden of proving that he has the right to these shares that my mother has bequeathed him.

Lawyer: Well, well—not quite, not quite. He has the burden to show that he didn't exert undue influence, because remember we're doing the undue influence thing. I told you it's about the undue influence.

Hearn: So he has the burden to show that he—so we don't have any burdens, like what's our burden? Where's the shifting?

Lawyer: Kind of. . .I mean, kind of. He's got the burden and then it shifts to us.

Hearn: He's got the burden to prove that he didn't exert undue influence, that's what you're telling me? He didn't do any—

Lawyer: Yep, he's got that fiduciary obligation, mm-hmm. He does, mm-hmm.

Hearn: Okay. So, all right—

Lawyer: Yeah, that's what he's got, yep. Mm-hmm.

6.5 What are the deficiencies of this legal explanation? Does the lawyer clarify the legal burdens each party bears? Does the lawyer explain the significance of the burdens to the client's chances of defeating the second will?

What are the risks of not providing a clear legal explanation to a client? How might the lawyer explain the law more effectively? Does the lawyer's legal explanation raise questions regarding the lawyer's compliance with ethical and professional standards?

Hearn: Okay, so he has to, like—the ball's in his court first and then it gets passed to us once he meets his burden.

Lawyer: Kind of, but it's more complicated than that but, I get it, you're not a lawyer, I get it.

Hearn: Okay. So what's the complication? Tell me about the comp—

Lawyer: It's just complicated. I wouldn't expect you to have any idea about this very, kind of, very complex—there's this thing called "burden shifting," there's presumptions, there's, um, there's balancing tests, you know, there are things called prima facie cases—all Latin, you know, it—it's complicated, it's very, very complicated. Very high-level, um—

Hearn: Okay, just tell me what it is.

Lawyer: It's, you know, it's just—it's, it's, it's, it's lawyer talk and—

Hearn: Uh huh.

Lawyer: —you know, with all due respect—you've really accomplished a lot but, you know, I'm the lawyer, let me do my lawyer thing.

6.6 What does the lawyer's statement of "let me do my lawyer thing" communicate to the client about the lawyer's view of their roles in resolving the client's problem? What does it communicate about the legal profession? About the client's capacity for understanding her situation and participating in the decision-making process?

Hearn: Right, right, right, but you're saying "we," so you want us to work together—

Lawyer: Yes!

Hearn: —and I really need to understand your—

Lawyer: But my job is to take your kind of layperson—kinda more simplistic way of saying something, and I—

Hearn: So just explain. Explain this to me.

Lawyer: —that I put it in language that the, that lawyers understand and that's how I get the great results. Anyway, um, okay—

Hearn: Can you provide like a, you know, a bulleted one-pager with your theory, please?

Lawyer: Well, that's a good idea, you know, but my, um, my summer intern is going back to college but, um—

Hearn: Can you do it? Can you just do it?

Lawyer: No that's a really good idea, uh, I'll definitely—you know what, this is what we say in the law: I'll take it under advisement. How's that? Okay?

6.7 Is the client's request for a "bulleted one-pager" reasonable? How does a lawyer determine what materials to prepare and share with the client during a counseling session? What are the advantages and disadvantages of preparing and showing the client a brief document or screen setting out the options for addressing the client's legal issue and the lawyer's assessment of the pros and cons of each option?

What does the lawyer's reference to her "summer intern" reveal about the lawyer's business model? Does her practice raise ethical concerns?

Hearn: Alright.

Lawyer: Um, so thi—but, um, I just need you to fight—you've told me that you've, you've, um, admitted the will. You filed an application to have the will admitted, you told me that?

Hearn: Mm-hmm.

Lawyer: I now know that. That's good! And so we're gonna go with the undue influence theory.

Hearn: Could you just go a little bit into what the other options could be and some of the pros and cons, so that we can choose the, the best path forward together? I've never been in a meeting where I don't have materials to markup and to look at and to give feedback to.

Lawyer: You know I think it's cuz you're much younger than I am and I just—this is, you're just gonna have to—you're, okay a digital native. I'm a digital immigrant. But I think in all fairness I have a lot to bring to this conversation.

Hearn: Okay you know what? Like, I can't believe you just brought that—I, I am literally your client. I pay you for your time.

Lawyer: I'm not trying to be patronizing cuz I'm twice your age. But I—but I am, and I actually—with that age I did—I wasn't just twiddling my thumbs. I was actually doing a lot of—I was studying and, and then I was trying cases and there was doing legal research and that's—you have to trust. It's back to that trust thing of, um—that, that I'm bringing up, and when I—I mean, you know what? This is all gonna get taken care of—

 6.8 What is the client expressing about her expectations for the counseling meeting? How does the client's view of her role in the legal decision-making differ from the lawyer's? In what ways has the lawyer failed to understand her client's interests and preferences? The lawyer refers to the difference in ages and digital familiarity between the client and herself. Are there other differences that may create barriers to communication? What cross-cultural communication techniques would overcome these barriers?

Hearn: Mm-hmm.

Lawyer: —it's gonna all get taken care of when I see the judge tonight. Don't even worry about it. I'm seeing Judge McGillicuddy in, um, for mah-jongg tonight. I'm gonna ask her everything, maybe we settle this all up.

Hearn: I just, I really don't want to do anything unethical here so I want to make sure that we're all above board here—

Lawyer: It's about relationships.

Hearn: Saying all of this to the judge and not being really clear, like, if I don't understand it, how—

Lawyer: So, don't worry about the judge.

Hearn: Okay.

Lawyer: So don't worry about the judge. I—so don't worry. You're in really good hands but, we're going with your idea. You know—

6.9 The client is troubled by the lawyer's plan to discuss her case with the judge at a social gathering. Does this raise ethical concerns? What does the lawyer's dismissive response communicate to the client about her decision-making authority?

Hearn: How are you gonna address, like, some of the concerns that you brought up to me last time? So that, ya know, this concern about the settlement that we reached with this alleged, um, you know, inappropriate, like, conversations or whatever?

Lawyer: That doesn't have anything—don't even worry about that.

Hearn: Okay. Alright.

Lawyer: Don't even worry about it. I don't even—I don't know why you're bringing it up.

Hearn: You were making such a big deal about it so that's why I thought it might be, you know, useful to touch base on.

Lawyer: Well, I think you were a little touchy about it, is what— I don't think, I don't—we, we recall things a little differently but, anyway—

Hearn: Uh huh.

Lawyer: —I don't want to waste, uh, your time.

Hearn: Yeah I, I really don't have a lot of time. I have a company to run.

Lawyer: But I really, really like this way. It's gonna be really good and we're gonna go with, um, uh, the undue influence that Dr. Snow—

6.10 The lawyer and client have different recollections of their earlier discussion regarding the client's settlement of sexual harassment claims in her family business. Should the lawyer involve the client in a discussion of whether and how the sexual harassment claims may affect the client's legal position? Compare the lawyer's dismissal of the client's concerns about the sexual harassment claims with how the lawyer addresses the same issue in Hearn Counseling 2. What does the lawyer risk by not revisiting this issue before the lawyer proceeds with a lawsuit?

Hearn: Do you think that there are any other options that we should be looking at right now? You know I, I had proposed a couple different ideas and then you attacked my ideas and you said that it wasn't very strong, and so I thought, you know, maybe you had some, done some other research and based on what you found maybe you had some. . .

Lawyer: Well, yeah, we've done a lot of research, um, and—

Hearn: And did you find any other solutions?

Lawyer: Well, um, you asked me do I think there are other options. In fact I know there are no other options—there are no other options.

Hearn: So what—what's my role in this?

Lawyer: You're a client. Um—

Hearn: Okay.

Lawyer: —and, um, you know you might have to say something like, "I think that there's a will. I think that it—there's a second will." Um. . .

6.11 How does the lawyer's casual mention that the client may have to testify at the hearing reflect a failure to engage in client-centered counseling? What may be the consequences of this conduct for the lawyer-client relationship, and ultimately, the client's case?

Hearn: Well, my concern is that I already admitted the will. Does that mean that, like, there's a, you know, that now I'm, I'm saying that the will should not be—that the will is unenforceable?

Lawyer: Wait.

Hearn: Can you just describe your—oh my god. . .

Lawyer: When did you send it?

Hearn: Um, I sent it right away last time, you know, after we met.

Lawyer: Hold on, hold on. I hate that little circle thing, you know, it's like stuck—

Hearn: Can, can I just take a look at this? Since you've drafted something here. . .I mean—

Lawyer: Actually, it's, you know, it, it's kind of, it's work product that in—we have—

Hearn: That we have generated together. There's like confidentiality—

Lawyer: There's something—well it's called lawyer work product and, um, there's just—it's, it's protected and no offense.

Hearn: For me!

Lawyer: Oh, here we go! Here we go. Okay. Wait, this is—there's a hearing. . .

Hearn: I'm literally working, you know, 80 hours a week and then I come to meet with you in my very few moments—

Lawyer: So, so it looks like—okay. So it looks like—okay, looks like next Wednesday there's going to be a meeting. An initial— a status conference—

Hearn: Okay.

Lawyer: —before Judge McGillicuddy. We're all set! We're good. We are so good. This is gonna—you're gonna really like this. It's gonna be a great result. See you on Wednesday, in the probate court, and we'll go from there.

Hearn: Okay, there's nothing else that I need to send you, or verify, or. . .

Lawyer: How about this, I'll tell you if there is. Okay?

Hearn: Okay, great. Yeah.

Lawyer: But it could come—just keep everything. I've got your text, I've got your email, you know I tend to be—I work really— I'm kind of I, I work very feverishly. I do my best work kind of in a crunch, you know? And so you could get something, like, at 2:00 in the morning, so. You keep late hours anyway, so—

Hearn: Right.

Lawyer: Um, just keep everything, every device on at all times.

Hearn: Hm.

Lawyer: Okay?

 6.12 What assumptions is the lawyer making about the client? To what extent may differences between the two be driving these assumptions? Does the lawyer's description of her workstyle raise ethical and professional issues? Based on her body language, how would you describe the client's emotions at the end of the meeting? Review some of the lawyer-client exchanges where the lawyer's conduct impairs the lawyer-client relationship. If you were the lawyer, how would you approach these exchanges in a way designed to create and maintain a productive lawyer-client relationship and meet the needs of the client?

Hearn: Okay.

Lawyer: Thank you! Thanks so much. Okay?

Hearn: Okay.

Lawyer: We're gonna do great.

Hearn: Alright.

Lawyer: Okay. Take care. Bye!

Hearn: Bye.

The End

CHAPTER 10

HEARN COUNSELING 2

You are about to watch a lawyer conduct a counseling meeting with client Jamie Hearn. Hearn has already met with the lawyer for an initial interview and is now returning to the lawyer's office to discuss legal options and decide on a course of action. As you observe the counseling meeting, note how the lawyer chooses to conduct the meeting and the impact of those choices on the client. Consider alternative approaches and techniques the lawyer could have used, and how you would have conducted this counseling meeting had you been the lawyer. Also consider the extent to which differences between the lawyer and client—differences in race, ethnicity, gender and age—may impact the dynamics between the lawyer and client.

DISCUSSION QUESTIONS

The following discussion questions highlight specific issues raised in this meeting. The timestamps indicate moments when you may pause the video to consider the questions and gauge your reactions to the lawyer-client conversation.

1:44: What steps does the lawyer take at the beginning of the meeting to build rapport and prepare for the transition to a substantive discussion? Is there more the lawyer could do at the outset to make the client comfortable? How well does the lawyer explain the purpose of the meeting and the client's role?

Before proceeding to counseling, the lawyer reviews the client's goals and checks on any new developments in the client's situation. What are the risks of failing to confirm the client's goals before proceeding to counseling?

5:45: How clear and effective is the lawyer's explanation of the legal standards governing the will dispute? Does the lawyer explain the legal standards in terms of the client's situation? Does the client seem to understand the technical terms being used? What steps could the lawyer take to confirm the client's understanding?

When the client asks whether the fact that his mother "may have been deceived by Dr. Snow" would demonstrate undue influence, is the lawyer's response adequate? Should the lawyer deviate from her explanation of the law to question the client about the basis for this theory? What are the advantages and disadvantages of doing so?

7:41: The lawyer asks the client how he feels about his ability to provide proof of testamentary capacity through documents and witnesses. Is it clear that the client understands what such documents and witnesses must say? In what ways might the lawyer provide the client with more guidance about what kinds of proof he should be prepared to provide?

The client raises the possibility of adverse testimony from an employee who did not sign a confidentiality agreement. How does the lawyer involve the client in the assessment of that possibility and future decision-making about how and when the employment claims against the client will be addressed in the case?

8:36: The lawyer lays out a number of options for the client and invites him to decide how to proceed. Has the lawyer provided sufficient guidance regarding the risks and opportunities associated with each option?

FOR FURTHER DISCUSSION

1. In what ways does the lawyer's nonverbal conduct help to maintain rapport and encourage client participation in the counseling process? How is the physical setting conducive to lawyer-client interaction?

2. How involved is the client in the discussion of law, the evaluation of the options and the decision about how to proceed?

3. The client chooses the option of probating the first will because he wants "closure." Is it clear that he has chosen the best option for providing "closure"? Should the lawyer offer guidance as to which option she believes is the best suited to accomplish the client's goals? What are the advantages and disadvantages of a lawyer offering a recommendation?

4. What techniques does the lawyer use to engender client comfort and confidence in the process and plan?

5. In what ways does the lawyer demonstrate a directive, client-centered or collaborative approach to client counseling?

ANNOTATED TRANSCRIPT

This annotated transcript is designed to be read as you watch the corresponding video. The annotations pose questions about the use, purpose and effect of various lawyering techniques; suggest issues for reflection; and highlight comparisons and contrasts among the different lawyering approaches featured in the videos.

Lawyer: Jamie, thank you for coming back in.

Hearn: Good to see you.

Lawyer: Hopefully, you know, things are starting to calm down a little bit for you with uh, dealing with everything with the business and the funeral. . .

Hearn: Yeah, all of the funeral arrangements, all that's behind us now and business is on a good footing right now. Stable, but obviously we've got a sort of cloud hanging over us a little bit with the, the probate issues.

Lawyer: So this is why I asked you to come back in because I wanted to talk about that a little bit and see what sort of what direction we want to go in.

Hearn: Sure.

Lawyer: So I've had the chance to review the documents since our last meeting, sort of gone through some of the facts and some of the timeline, and thank you for sending everything over and in a timely fashion. Here are, um, some of the things that are going to be relevant, and so what I want to do is I'm going to tell you a little bit about, sort of, what's the law behind it and why we're thinking about these things and then we'll talk about how you want to proceed.

7.1 What tone does the lawyer set for the counseling meeting in these first few moments? What does the lawyer convey by explaining at the outset the structure and purpose of the counseling meeting, and client's role in it? Compare the lawyer's tone and statements at the beginning of this meeting with the lawyer's conduct at the beginning of Hearn Counseling 1. Which meeting is likely to result in higher client satisfaction? Why?

Hearn: Sure.

Lawyer: You can, of course, contest the second will which, based on our last session and our subsequent follow-up, I think is a direction you want to go in. But of course, tell me if I'm somehow, uh, wrong.

Hearn: No, absolutely, that's what I want to do is contest the second will in any way we can, um, legally.

Lawyer: Okay. Based on that we'll have to think about a couple of things. The first thing we'll have to think about is where the will is going to be contested, because the second will was executed in, in Florida and you were here in Connecticut. The company's here and it's headquartered here in Connecticut.

Hearn: Yes, ma'am.

Lawyer: So that'll be something that we'll have to decide, sort of, what's the best venue for us. But speaking to the law, exactly, behind the wills—you sort of need three things in order to make a valid will. The first thing, usually, is that you've got to be at least 18 years old, because you need to be an adult. And then you need testamentary capacity, and you need to not have any undue influence.

Hearn: Okay.

Lawyer: So the 18 or older is, is pretty easy. The other two are— have some nuances.

Hearn: Yes.

Lawyer: So, starting with the first one—testamentary capacity. That basically means that, um, the person making the will was sound in mind and memory.

Hearn: Right.

Lawyer: Enough so that they understood the decisions they were making, and that what they were doing was what they wanted to do.

Hearn: Okay.

Lawyer: The burden of proving, um, that the person had testamentary capacity is usually the person who is the proponent of the will. So in this case, we will be contesting the second will. It might get a little murky because you can't really leave out the first will by contesting the second will. Try to think of it more in terms of, you're advocating the first will. So you want—we will have to prove that your mom had testamentary capacity when she made the first will.

Hearn: Okay.

Lawyer: If Michael Snow is pursuing the same—is advocating that the second will is the valid one, then it will be his burden to prove that she had testamentary capacity at the time she made the second will. Sometimes something is not quite your burden but maybe proving that the first will is valid is one of, kind of, our strategic outlooks in trying to invalidate the second will.

Hearn: Okay.

Lawyer: There is a presumption of sanity when somebody takes an action, so we will really have to show whether there's anything that would undermine that at the time—

Hearn: Okay. . .

Lawyer: —the second will was made. And so to do that, we will look at her conduct and circumstances surrounding the execution of the second will, leading up to the time that was made and then what happened after. So factors like her accident, you know, the drugs that she was taking at the time, whether she was being isolated, uh, by, um, Snow and his foundation. There will also be some things about the relationship between you and her at the time, like would she have wanted to have changed her will.

Hearn: Okay.

Lawyer: Those are all things that we'll have to consider in that test. And secondly, then we'll have to look at whether, um, there was any undue influence. So maybe she had testamentary capacity but she was overwhelmed by undue influence. And what that means is that, basically, someone or something exerted so much pressure on her that they basically overcame her free agency.

Hearn: Okay.

Lawyer: She would not have made that decision if she was just left up to her own devices, so she was sort of, in some way, coerced or forced into making this decision.

Hearn: I have a question about that. Um, would the fact that she might have been deceived by Dr. Snow play into the, the undue influence piece?

Lawyer: It would. It, it—cause it all sort of goes to her mindset, it goes to her mental condition, and again we look at some of the things that happened before and the things that happen after, so. It didn't sound like there was anything physical, like she wasn't restrained, but, you know, those are things that we would look into. Like, was she free to leave if she wanted to? And, and so we'll be looking at things that would seem too coercive, something that would, sort of, exert some kind of a mind control over her. And if we can prove either that, a) she didn't have testamentary capacity, or even if she did but there was too much undue influence, then that's our avenue for invalidating the second will. Those are the things that we have to prove.

Hearn: Mm-hmm.

Lawyer: How do you feel about your ability to provide proof, whether it's in some of the documents that we've already seen, in getting people to testify in a trial about things leading up to her accident, things that happened after her accident, anyone with knowledge of all what was going on with her and Snow?

7.2 How effective is the lawyer's explanation of the legal principles governing testamentary capacity and undue influence? Why? How does this legal explanation compare with the explanation in Hearn Counseling 1? What are the advantages of describing to the client the kinds of evidence that will be needed to invalidate the second will, and inviting the client's input on whether and how that evidence can be secured?

Hearn: I think we'll be alright. I think there might be one person who might cause us some issues.

Lawyer: And who would that person be?

Hearn: That would be, um, one of the, uh, one of my employees who had a harassment complaint that did not sign a confidentiality agreement with me. Um—

Lawyer: Did that person have a relationship with your mother?

Hearn: He was just a tailor at one of the stores.

Lawyer: Did your mother spend a lot of time in the stores?

Hearn: Oh, not towards the end of her life, no. I mean, um—

Lawyer: What about before?

Hearn: A little bit, but it was really my Uncle Allen who was taking the lead on being in the stores. She dealt a lot with the store owners—

Lawyer: Okay.

Hearn: —not with the employees on a day-to-day basis.

Lawyer: Okay, so the value of his testimony might—it might not have much value.

Hearn: Yeah, I don't even know if the guy ever met my mother. But if they were, like, looking at my mother's motivations for why she might have changed her mind, if that comes up and if Dr. Snow—that guy knows anything about that situation they might bring it up but, um, it doesn't have, really, any bearing on, on my mother specifically.

Lawyer: Some of these claims, you know, they could have—they could factor in.

Hearn: Okay.

Lawyer: And so they're not something that we can ignore, but it's good that we know about them up—we know about them upfront so we can lay out our game plan, how we will address them, and whether it makes sense for us to raise them first or to sort of wait and see the approach that they're going to take. But those are—these are all decisions that, you know, we'll make along the way as we sort of see how our case is proceeding.

7.3 Is the lawyer obligated to consult with the client about the "game plan" once the client decides to pursue a lawsuit to contest his mother's bequest to Snow? Compare the lawyer's commitment to consult with the client about if and how to raise the harassment claims with the lawyer's dismissal of the client's concerns about the claims in Hearn Counseling 1. What are the advantages of involving the client in decisions about how the client's objectives will be achieved?

Hearn: Okay.

Lawyer: Um, what I want for you to do today is sort of decide, kind of, on our timing. Is this something that you want to jump into and start pursuing right away? Did you want to take a "wait-and-see" approach to see if he tries to assert the claim? Do you want to try probate in the first will first and see if he challenges it with the second will?

Hearn: I like that approach. Let's try to, um, probate. Let's try to execute that first will, you know, the one that I think is valid, and see if he comes up with a challenge or if, you know, everything's covered legally on our side and our will just goes through. Because I want to resolve this in some way. The "wait-and-see" makes me uncomfortable. You know, he could go after me. He could take control of the company with this, what I think is a dubious will.

7.4 Has the lawyer sufficiently counseled the client about these options? What more might the client need to know in order to make a decision? Should the lawyer provide her own recommendation based on the client's stated objectives? What are the advantages and disadvantages of a lawyer making a recommendation?

Lawyer: So the one thing that I've done before this meeting was to double-check, uh, the courts in Florida to make sure that the second will hadn't been brought before the courts, and that's simply what it means when I say, "probate the will," is to have a court kind of bless it as, you know, sort of, this is the real will. And, so far, nothing's been filed in Florida.

Hearn: Okay.

Lawyer: So we'll proceed with, um, sort of taking the first will through court here and then we'll see, you know, what's the challenge that he raises and then we'll proceed from there. Sound good to you?

Hearn: Yes. No, no, that sounds good to me. I think that's the option that we should pursue, um, because like I said I want to get something moving. I, I want to get some sort of closure. Clarity. Um, it's been a difficult time for me and my family and, um, and for the business, and I want to ensure as little disruption due to this will issue as possible. So I, I like that approach, I like that plan very much.

Lawyer: Well, we'll proceed with that. I'll start drafting up some of documents that we'll need and I'll have you come back in so that we can have another opportunity to, um, to talk about them, to review them, and then we'll start moving forward.

Hearn: Alright, sounds good to me.

Lawyer: Okay, thank you so much for coming in.

Hearn: Thank you very much.

The End

If you are assigned or otherwise plan to role-play the counseling of Mic Snow, do not read beyond this page until you have completed the simulation.

CHAPTER 11

SNOW COUNSELING 1

You are about to watch a lawyer conduct a counseling meeting with client Mic Snow. Snow has already met with the lawyer for an initial interview and is now returning to the lawyer's office to discuss legal options and decide on a course of action. As you observe the counseling meeting, note how the lawyer chooses to conduct the meeting and the impact of those choices on the client. Consider alternative approaches and techniques the lawyer could have used, and how you would have conducted this counseling meeting had you been the lawyer. Also consider the extent to which differences between the lawyer and client—differences in race, ethnicity, gender and age—may impact the dynamics between the lawyer and client.

DISCUSSION QUESTIONS

The following discussion questions highlight specific issues raised in this meeting. The timestamps indicate moments when you may pause the video to consider the questions and gauge your reactions to the lawyer-client conversation.

0:57: What steps does the lawyer take to establish rapport? What more could the lawyer say or do at the beginning of the meeting to make the client comfortable and encourage her participation?

Within the first minute of the meeting, the lawyer informs the client that she will have difficulty winning a lawsuit. Is this the optimal time and way to deliver this news to the client? Why or why not? What is the effect of this news on the client? How might the lawyer preface this news so that the client is prepared to hear it and understands the basis for the lawyer's conclusion?

3:19: How clear is the lawyer's explanation of the law regarding testamentary capacity? Does the lawyer's legal explanation support his conclusion that Ms. Hearn lacked testamentary capacity to make the bequest to Snow's foundation? Is the lawyer's legal conclusion based on an objective analysis of the facts? To what extent does the lawyer's perception of the client's "experimental treatments" influence his assessment of her legal claim? How might the lawyer invite the client's input into the issue of whether the Khoo Yaa Daa therapy could impair judgment or cognitive capacity?

The lawyer expresses that he was "shocked" when the client described her treatment techniques. How does the lawyer's reaction affect the maintenance of rapport and open communication between the lawyer and client? What are the risks of lawyers reacting to client disclosures in an emotional and/or judgmental way?

5:18: How well does the lawyer explain the law of undue influence? Is the explanation related to the client's situation? What might the client contribute to the assessment of her legal position? How can the lawyer invite greater participation by the client?

8:08: The lawyer lays out two options for resolving the dispute with Ms. Hearn's son: settlement and going to trial. When discussing trial, the lawyer acknowledges that the client does not want to try the case and the lawyer "wouldn't want that either." What are the risks and benefits of telling a client what the lawyer would do in the client's position?

How well does the lawyer explain the option of settlement? What does the client's reaction to the prospect of an "immediate" settlement reveal about her understanding of the lawyer's assessment of her case? Has the lawyer adequately prepared the client to make an informed decision about whether and on what basis to settle?

FOR FURTHER DISCUSSION

1. How would you describe the lawyer's body language throughout the meeting? What do the lawyer's facial expressions reveal about his attitudes toward the client and her case?

2. The lawyer takes a negative view of the case at the beginning of the meeting, and his assessment becomes more dire as the meeting progresses. Does the lawyer adequately explain the reasons for his pessimism? What effect does the lawyer's increasingly grim view have on the client, the lawyer's legal conclusions and the decision-making process?

3. Consider the level of client participation in the meeting as it progresses. To what extent does the lawyer's conduct at the outset of the meeting affect how the client participates— either by asking questions or providing information— throughout the rest of the meeting?

4. Late in the meeting, the lawyer advises the client—for the first time—that she should be worried about her own assets. How effectively does the lawyer explain the reason for his warning? What is the effect of this news on the client and her ability to make an informed decision about how to proceed? How could the lawyer more effectively respond to the client's obvious distress over her potential legal exposure?

5. To what extent does the lawyer present options to the client and invite her input into assessing their risks and benefits? To what extent does the lawyer obtain the client's authorization for him to pursue a course of action on the client's behalf? What is the nature of the authority the lawyer obtains to call Hearn's lawyer immediately following that meeting to start settlement negotiations? What are the risks of rushing a client into making a decision?

6. Should a lawyer come up with a variety of options for a client even if the lawyer believes that there is only one option that meets the client's goals? What are the risks of failing to consider or present other possibilities?

7. Describe the client's demeanor at the end of the meeting? How would you feel if you were the client? When a lawyer senses at the close of a meeting that a client is dissatisfied with the result, what is an effective response? What are the risks of pursuing a course of action with which the client is unhappy?

8. In what ways does the lawyer demonstrate a directive,
    client-centered or collaborative approach to client
    counseling?

ANNOTATED TRANSCRIPT

This annotated transcript is designed to be read as you watch the corresponding video. The annotations pose questions about the use, purpose and effect of various lawyering techniques; suggest issues for reflection; and highlight comparisons and contrasts among the different lawyering approaches featured in the videos.

Lawyer: Dr. Snow, thanks for coming in. Good to see you again.

Snow: Hi there.

Lawyer: So, in the, uh, last few days I've had a chance to review the law as we talked about in, um, in the first meeting we had, and I want to walk you through, uh, some of my conclusions, uh, about your, about your issue. So, you talked about, uh, in the last time wanting to avoid, um, basically wanting to avoid a lawsuit.

Snow: Yes.

Lawyer: And so, um, you know, I just have to tell you that, based on my preliminary research, um, that looks like, uh, if there is indeed a lawsuit, something that we may have difficulty winning. Okay?

Snow: Oh.

Lawyer: So, I know that's probably not the news that you wanted to hear, um, but, uh, I have some, um, some ideas and actually some, I think some guidance that I can give you as to what I think your next steps should be. Okay?

 8.1 What efforts does the lawyer make to reestablish rapport with the client at the outset of the meeting? How might the lawyer structure the counseling meeting so as to prepare the client for his assessment of her legal situation and to facilitate collaborative decision-making?

Snow: Okay.

Lawyer: So, uh, in terms of the, the actual law on the issue, um, there's a lot of cases, um, that illustrate a couple of things that I think, based on your description of the facts, we'll, we'll have difficulty with: testamentary capacity, I'll explain what that is in a second—

Snow: Okay.

Lawyer: —and then also undue influence. And so, um, in terms of testamentary capacity, uh, you know, we talked about in the last meeting, um, some of the experimental treatments that you were using—

Snow: Yes. . .

Lawyer: —um, with the people, the, the addiction—folks that were suffering from addiction. And so, the idea that, um, of testamentary capacity is that the person making out the will, okay, actually has the mental capability to understand what they're doing and to, um, sort of, um, sign in a way that's meaningful, right? That they're actually conveying their estate and their assets, uh, in a way that they understand.

Snow: Okay.

Lawyer: There's no, sort of, set test for this, um, but basically what it comes down to, in my judgment, is that you've, um, been treating Ms. Hearn, um, by, um, as we discussed, you know, and I was fairly shocked, uh, to hear the, you know, um, electricity? Or the, the, sort of—

Snow: Yes. Mm-hmm.

Lawyer: —pulses into her, into her brain. You described that, um, which I think creat—first of all, creates just kind of a very, um, murky context to testamentary capacity, right? Um, particularly since you said that the will was executed right around a treatment or in close proximity to, to one of her treatments. And, in fact, that she died, um, not all that long after this occurred. So, while, um, you know, we're still going to advocate, um, for you if, if, you know, to the extent possible and if you'd like to go forward, I do think that there's very much a murky question around this. And so, um, this idea of testamentary capacity, that is, and whether Ms. Hearn really had the, the ability, uh, and the capability to execute this will, um, that we have, um, uh, as the subject of, of, of this dispute basically. So, that's the first thing.

8.2 The lawyer states that he "was fairly shocked" to learn of Snow's treatment techniques and suggests that they raise a "murky" issue of testamentary capacity. How might the lawyer's perception of the Khoo Yaa Daa therapy affect the lawyer-client relationship and the quality of the lawyer's legal counsel?

The second thing is undue influence, okay? And so, undue influence is basically, um, you know, someone in a position of trust like, right, that you were basically in this instance. You're not a medical doctor but you're certainly a professional providing her treatment, um, may have, you know, just to make it very basic, unduly influenced the person giving their estate. Right? There's sort of some very murky, very murky, um, I think, facts around that for us as well, given your relationship to Ms. Hearn and also given the fact that, in, in my view and based on your descriptions, she really maybe didn't fully understand the treatment? We'd have to look at the releases and everything else that you say that she signed, but, um, you know, there's sort of a question that's raised right away with undue influence about, um, you know, whether she might have made a different disposition. And, in fact, she did have a different will, you said, beforehand. Right?

Snow: Mm-hmm. Mm-hmm, yes.

Lawyer: Also, there's going to be a question, uh, I think with the undue influence, of the fact that you said you were one of the witnesses.

Snow: Yes.

Lawyer: So, um, you were clearly there, um, you know, she had just had a treatment, um, so whether or not she even had the testamentary capacity in the first place, but whether you were trying to influence her to, um, to give away her, her money. You said you could use it, um, but that you didn't need to, so that would certainly be a fact that would be helpful for us. That, you know, you do, you do have quite a bit of money, um—

Snow: Yes.

Lawyer: —and, you know, we could certainly argue that maybe, you know, you didn't need, uh, to have her money, right. So, um, there's not sort of that that undue influence. Okay? So, just from a legal standpoint, I wanted to highlight those two issues, um, as ones that I don't think are helpful—

Snow: Okay.

8.3 How well does the lawyer explain the law and its application to the client's situation? Does the client seem to understand the lawyer's legal explanation? What might the lawyer do to ensure that the client understands the law and is fully aware of the facts on which the lawyer bases his assessment of her case?

Lawyer: —for you. Um, the, um, the terms of the options. So, you said avoiding a lawsuit, so you have the option of settling a case at any time.

Snow: What is that? What does that mean?

Lawyer: Settling is, um, basically coming to a compromise where both sides get something, usually. And the plaintiff or whoever's initiating the lawsuit agrees to withdraw it based on that compromise. So, if you think about this case, right, that would mean that probably Ms. Hearn's son is going to get some money—usually it's money—okay? Um, and, um, would agree not to sue or to withdraw the suit as a way to avoid, obviously, a trial and avoid the matter altogether. Um, so settlement is clearly an option. Going to trial is clearly an option as well, though you've said that you don't want that.

Snow: No.

Lawyer: Um, I would say I wouldn't want that either. Um, I don't think, um, I really don't think that there's much, um, of an ability to, to win this case. Um, so I wouldn't advise that at all.

Snow: Okay.

Lawyer: And so, that's where I think you, you really should be, you really should be going.

Snow: But I thought, in our initial discussion, you thought that my, my claims were pretty good.

Lawyer: Yeah, but what, what you described, uh, in, in our discussion, um, in terms of the treatment that you had given to Ms. Hearn, and then the fact that you were there, uh, and you signed the will, um, these are things that are very, very bad for you. And so, you really do, you need to settle this and you need to do it immediately.

8.4 The lawyer tells the client that she must settle the matter "immediately." How does this dire warning compare with what the lawyer tells the client at the beginning of the counseling meeting? How would a more structured meeting prevent the client from being blindsided by the lawyer's advice? Has the lawyer adequately counseled the client about her options? To what extent does the lawyer involve the client in the decision-making?

Snow: But it's, it's the principle of the thing. I mean, she, she wanted this money to go to this foundation, so that we could push this.

Lawyer: And, you know, as we talked about before, um, you know, you were doing things to her that I, frankly, question whether she really understood what she wanted. And so, that's my point about testamentary capacity, right? And, and her ability to understand what, what she was doing when she executed this will. And so, you need to settle this with the son right away.

Snow: But then he would get, he would get everything and I would just get nothing?

Lawyer: Well, I'm going to fight to get you as much as I possibly can, but—

Snow: Well what does that mean?

Lawyer: Well, that means that whatever I can get in a negotiation with the son is, is—

Snow: Okay, but that wouldn't be a trial, that would be different?

Lawyer: That's not a trial at all. So, what we're gonna do is take her assets, essentially. Um, we're going to divide them up in a compromise, right? Um, so hopefully we'll get something out of that and the son will obviously get something as well, and then he'll agree not to sue you.

Snow: Okay.

Lawyer: That's what we'll do.

Snow: Okay. And, and now you're making me concerned about him possibly trying to get more. Is there any way to protect the rest of my foundation's assets? Is there any way to protect this process? I, I. . .

Lawyer: Well, I think that you re—you know, the foundation is one thing, but it sounds like, from our last meeting, you should really be worried about your own assets. You said you had "billions," was the term you used.

Snow: Yes, yes.

Lawyer: So, I would definitely be more worried about that money than your foundation's money. And so, you know, what we're gonna—what we'll do, I'm going to call the son, alright? Ms. Hearn's son. I'm going to tell him that we want to settle this matter. I'm going to do it quickly so that, hopefully, he doesn't even understand, uh, the possibilities that he might have, to go after you for his mother's death—

 8.5 The lawyer raises for the first time that the client's personal assets may be at risk. Does the lawyer provide the client with sufficient information to evaluate this risk?

Snow: Okay.

Lawyer: —and we'll, we'll be done with the matter right away.

Snow: This is such a mess, such a mess. But that's really the best thing?

Lawyer: Not only the best, it's what you have to do. There's really no other.

Snow: That's my only option?

Lawyer: It's the only option that I can see.

Snow: Okay. Okay. You've given me a lot to think about.

Lawyer: Okay, so I'm gonna go call the son right away.

Snow: Oh. Right, right now?

Lawyer: Like as soon as you leave.

Snow: Okay. Okay.

Lawyer: You need to do this.

Snow: Okay. So I have to decide right now?

Lawyer: Yes.

Snow: Oh, okay. Um, okay. I guess, I guess you're telling me that's my only option, I guess that's the only thing I can do.

Lawyer: If you want to avoid a suit, um—

Snow: Yes, I need to avoid a suit.

Lawyer: —and protect your money, this is, this is the only option you really have.

 8.6 Compare this counseling meeting with Hearn Counseling 1. In what ways do the lawyers take similar approaches to counseling? How do they differ? Is the client's decision to pursue an immediate settlement with Hearn the product of a client-centered decision-making process? How might the lawyer respond to the client's concerns about the option presented? How might the decision-making process impact the client's satisfaction with the representation and her willingness to abide by a settlement negotiated on her behalf?

Snow: Okay. Okay.

Lawyer: Okay. Thank you.

Snow: Thank you.

The End

CHAPTER 12

SNOW COUNSELING 2

You are about to watch a lawyer conduct a counseling meeting with client Mic Snow. Snow has already met with the lawyer for an initial interview and is now returning to the lawyer's office to discuss legal options and decide on a course of action. As you observe the counseling meeting, note how the lawyer chooses to conduct the meeting and the impact of those choices on the client. Consider alternative approaches and techniques the lawyer could have used, and how you would have conducted this counseling meeting had you been the lawyer. Also consider the extent to which differences between the lawyer and client—differences in race, ethnicity, gender and age—may impact the dynamics between the lawyer and client.

DISCUSSION QUESTIONS

The following discussion questions highlight specific issues raised in this meeting. The timestamps indicate moments when you may pause the video to consider the questions and gauge your reactions to the lawyer-client conversation.

2:29: What steps does the lawyer take at the beginning of the meeting to build rapport and facilitate communication? Are there additional steps the lawyer could take to make the client comfortable? How does the lawyer respond to the client's statement that she is feeling "anxious"? How might the lawyer make an active listening response to that statement? How do the lawyer's tone and body language contribute to maintenance of rapport and open communication? Is the lawyer's description of the attorney-client privilege accurate? What is the effect of the lawyer's focus on how that privilege could be lost?

The lawyer repeats the client's primary goal, and then asks about any other goals the client might have. Is this an effective way of asking if the client's goals have changed? When the client mentions that she had not given other goals much thought, should the lawyer have offered more guidance on how she might do that? How and why?

The lawyer reiterates that the client is in the "driver's seat" with regard to the overall direction of the case. He also states that it is a "partnership" between the lawyer and client to get the best result. Is this an accurate representation of the lawyer-client relationship? Is the lawyer's approach consistent with his role as he describes it?

7:31: How clearly does the lawyer explain the legal terms, standards and burdens of proof relevant to the client's case? Does he explain the law in terms of the client's situation? How does the lawyer's analysis reflect his understanding of Snow's healing practices and relationship with Ms. Hearn?

The lawyer's legal explanation is an uninterrupted four-minute monologue. How engaged is the client while the lawyer is talking? What is the risk of the lawyer speaking at length without inviting client participation? How might the lawyer encourage the client to ask questions or express opinions? What nonverbal cues from the client should the lawyer be looking for when determining whether to continue talking or to pause for the client to interject?

9:26: How clearly and thoroughly does the lawyer answer the client's question about "what happens next"? When the lawyer describes summary judgment and why he might make that motion during litigation, does the client appear to understand? What might a lawyer do to confirm that the client is following a legal explanation?

FOR FURTHER DISCUSSION

1. In what ways does the lawyer's tone and conduct help to maintain rapport and encourage client participation in the counseling process? How is the physical setting conducive to lawyer-client interaction?

2. How well does the lawyer organize the meeting? What is the value of the lawyer communicating the meeting structure to the client as he moves from one topic to another?

3. The lawyer provides the client a description of how litigation would proceed, but does the lawyer explore options outside of litigation? Does the lawyer review the pros and cons of the options and invite client input in assessing them? What are the risks of failing to evaluate the options?

4. Does the lawyer fully address the client's concerns regarding the potential damage to the reputation of her business if Hearn goes "to the press"? Does the client explain the reason for her concerns? What additional issues might the lawyer want to investigate and counsel the client about in this regard?

5. In what ways does the lawyer demonstrate a directive, client-centered or collaborative approach to client counseling?

ANNOTATED TRANSCRIPT

This annotated transcript is designed to be read as you watch the corresponding video. The annotations pose questions about the use, purpose and effect of various lawyering techniques; suggest issues for reflection; and highlight comparisons and contrasts among the different lawyering approaches featured in the videos.

Lawyer: Welcome back. Pleasure to see you again.

Snow: Thank you.

Lawyer: So, how have you been?

Snow: Uh, I've been fine. I'm obviously a little anxious, um, but, but, everything is going fine.

Lawyer: Okay. It's been, what, two weeks since we last spoke?

Snow: Yes.

 9.1 What efforts does the lawyer make to reestablish rapport with the client at the outset of the meeting? Does the lawyer make an active listening response to the client's statement about being anxious? Is there a risk to his approach?

Lawyer: Okay. And in that time I've, uh, I've done a little, a little research. Um, thank you for getting back to me with the, uh, the signed retainer agreement. I just wanted to bring you up to speed as to what I've been doing and how the case is shaping up.

Snow: Okay.

Lawyer: Let me first touch upon any other goals that you may have. I mean, the goal that her, her intent and her will be carried forward and carried out, that is a primary goal. But are there any other things that I should be thinking about as I go along in this case?

9.2 The lawyer begins the meeting by confirming the client's goals. What are the advantages of beginning a counseling session in this way? Are there ways in which the lawyer could improve the beginning of the meeting?

Snow: No. That's obviously something I need to make sure I think about and also communicate with you every step of the way.

Lawyer: Yes. I still want you to keep looking for any documents, any anything that, that has the back and forth between you, uh, and Ms. Hearn, because even something that might seem insignificant to you could be very helpful to our case—or hurtful—and I need to know both of those things.

Snow: Okay.

Lawyer: I want to reiterate what I said before about attorney-client privilege: what you say to me and, and what I say to you in, in terms of giving legal advice is privileged. That being said, some people want to go out and talk about their case; I would encourage you not to do that. Because, although the privilege exists between us, you can break that privilege by going and talking to other people, by telling them about what we talked about, because those people, that's not a privileged conversation usually.

Snow: No matter what happens in all of this, my, my first concern has to be that my business and the reputation of my business does not suffer through this.

Lawyer: So, I would—I strongly advise you not to talk about the case to anyone else, um, other than me, at least while it's ongoing. I want to reiterate for you that you are in the driver's seat with regard to what we do in terms of the overall direction of the case. And so it's, it's sort of a partnership, it is a partnership between you and I to get the best result and outcome for you. Okay, I'm going to shift gears now and we'll talk about a little of, of what I've come up with as far as the research, and if at any point you're unclear about any of the terms I'm using—

I'll try and steer clear of the so-called "legalese"—um, but it would help if you know what the terms are, so that, that if you hear them again in the future you know what I'm talking about or what someone else is talking about. So, there's something called "testamentary capacity." Basically, could this person enter into a will? What matters there is, who's got to prove that? And that's an "us" type question, and what I mean by that is, we've got the burden of showing that Ms. Hearn had the ability to make a will. That doesn't mean that she had to be absolutely physically fit, at the top of her game, that's not what that means. It just means she knew what was going on and she didn't have to have even the ability to run a whole company or so forth. Though, in this case we have some good facts, right?

9.3 What does the lawyer's statement that the client "is in the driver's seat" reveal about the lawyer's approach to counseling and his view of the allocation of responsibility between lawyer and client? In what ways does the counseling that follows adhere to principles of collaborative or client-centered counseling?

Snow: Yes, we do.

Lawyer: She was back up on her feet, running her company, um, and so that looks, that looks like it's something that goes in the—into the positive column, keeping in mind that we would have to prove that, um, but it's not a huge haul. Shifting over to what will be a huge haul, I think, for the other side—"undue influence." Basically, that you were a Svengali, that you had Ms. Hearn under your spell and she couldn't resist doing exactly what it was you wanted, and that exact thing would have been to turn over all of her worldly possessions with the exception of a few crumbs to her children. Right? That's how you're going to be painted, but that's a "them" type proposition, something they will have to show. And usually in cases like this, civil cases, it's "preponderance of the evidence," it's "more likely than not." That's usually the standard, but for undue influence, because the law disfavors people coming and going behind what is facially a valid will, the law puts an extra, sort of, burden on the other side. It's "clear and convincing evidence" so it's, it's a heightened burden, and that's good for us because the higher their burden is to prove something, the better chance that, that we do better in the end.

Snow: Mm-hmm.

Lawyer: But, there—and there is a "but" here—the type of relationship that you had with Ms. Hearn, um, if they can sort of shoehorn that into a relationship where you had some sort of psychological control over her, or some sort of a business or professional relationship, especially if it's, it's like a, uh, a psychiatrist or psychologist or someone like that who, who ordinarily would have that sort of control over someone, then that sort of shifts it back from a "them" to an "us" type situation. And I'm using very crude terms here, but you can see how that would make sense, right? If it's just, you know, one person who is presumed to have engaged in undue influence over another person, that's one thing. But if that other person has some sort of special relationship, then the law sort of pulls back and says, "well we're going to, we're going to look at that a little differently." And so your business, uh, the Khoo Yaa Daa business is sort of walking the line on both, uh, both sides, right? Your relationship with Ms. Hearn towards the end was one of a friendship relationship, but while you were dealing with her as a patient, you were both semi-medical—you're taking MRIs and doing baseline tests and so forth—and you're also, it also, um, has a spiritual component to your, um, your technique and your method of dealing with addiction. And so they're going to try and paint you into that light so that they can get away from their very heavy burden, um, under the undue influence portion of the case.

Snow: So it's, it's—I think the important distinction here, if we're faced with that, is that the "Khoo Yaa Daa" the chant portion, if you will, of this is mindfulness and self-awareness and it is not a religious fixation. To the extent that we can make that clear and, and that I can provide you with the information that you need to have at your disposal—

Lawyer: Yes.

Snow: —about that distinction. That's very important, I would think.

Lawyer: And I will, I will be mindful of that, and, and what, what you should know is that they, they will try and mix religion and religious type, um, situations with what here is more of a spiritual type, and they'll try and weave them together. If their lawyer is worth his or her salt, that'll be where they'll go because that's where I would go. So, do you have any, any other questions for me? Or anything you want me to elaborate on?

9.4 How well does the lawyer explain the law and its application to the client's situation? Compare the lawyer's presentation of the legal arguments and counter-arguments with the legal analysis offered by the lawyer in Snow Counseling 1. See note 8.3. How does each lawyer portray the facts that may pose challenges to the client's case? In what ways is this lawyer's approach more likely to maintain rapport with the client and invite the client's input into decisions about legal strategy?

Snow: I, I guess it's just the big question: What can I expect next? How often are we going to meet? Um, what happens next?

Lawyer: Sure. These types of cases, with undue influence, as I told you in our previous meeting are exceedingly fact-intensive: What did someone mean versus what did they say? When did it happen? And so the more you can create, uh, a dispute of material fact—a fact that really matters, you know, not, not was the carpet was blue or green but, you know, did Ms. Hearn have capacity or not. These types of questions, they require a trial. Um, though I will try to get it knocked out on summary judgment, that's, that's not a very likely outcome in a case such as this. But that doesn't mean that's not useful. It is, because sometimes summary judgment, just like other motions practice, can whittle down the case and maybe kick out one thing or another, and so it gives us less to focus on if we go to trial. And it also shows the other side, this is the evidence that you're up against, and so do you really want to go to trial on this or do you want to settle with me. Um, so it's got a few, a few reasons why you would do that to soften up the other side and get them in the position where they come to the table and we can work something out, because, again, working it out is the way most— the vast majority of these cases happen. A settlement is preferable to handing someone else, some group of strangers, your checkbook and saying, "you decide." That would not honor Ms. Hearn's memory or her wishes or be beneficial to you if we were to roll the dice. So cases often settle, um, that's just the way of the world in, in in the legal world, civil as well as criminal. So, have I answered all your questions?

9.5 Does the client have sufficient information to evaluate her options? What are the advantages of a lawyer inviting the client to have input into the assessment of the options? Does the client explicitly authorize the lawyer to pursue a particular course of action on her behalf?

Snow: Um, I think you have. I have a question for you about— and you've been very clear with me about not speaking about this at all and I understand that—um, what if they start speaking? What if they go to the press? How am I to react to that?

Lawyer: Then you—if you're asked for comment, then you say that, you know, you're not at liberty to speak about pending litigation. Right? You avoid engaging, right? Don't go for the bait and don't go for the head fakes here. Um, what they want is they want you to make a mistake, um, litigation in some instances is about either forcing or waiting for the other side to make mistakes and then we capitalize on them. It sounds, it sounds harsh and, and calculated and it is. But, you have to just weather the storm with this because they're going to apply pressure to you in any way they can. Do not succumb to that pressure. You let me be your mouthpiece. This is what I do, this is beneficial to you, and you speaking can only hurt our case.

Snow: Mm-hmm. Again, it goes to the reputation of my business. The more they talk, the more, the more damaging it is.

Lawyer: I would advise you strongly not to talk. Um, but if you want to talk about something then talk about how beneficial your business has been to people, and stick to that versus the facts of this particular case.

 9.6 Does the lawyer fully explore the client's concerns about the press? What are the risks of failing to understand the nature and source of these concerns?

Snow: Mm-hmm. Okay. Okay. Alright. Very good. Very good, thank you.

Lawyer: Alright, pleasure.

Snow: Thank you.

The End

CHAPTER 13

SNOW COUNSELING 3

You are about to watch a lawyer conduct a counseling meeting with client Mic Snow. Snow has already met with the lawyer for an initial interview and is now returning to the lawyer's office to discuss legal options and decide on a course of action. As you observe the counseling meeting, note how the lawyer chooses to conduct the meeting and the impact of those choices on the client. Consider alternative approaches and techniques the lawyer could have used, and how you would have conducted this counseling meeting had you been the lawyer. Also consider the extent to which differences between the lawyer and client—differences in race, ethnicity, gender and age—may impact the dynamics between the lawyer and client.

DISCUSSION QUESTIONS

The following discussion questions highlight specific issues raised in this meeting. The timestamps indicate moments when you may pause the video to consider the questions and gauge your reactions to the lawyer-client conversation.

1:10: What is the effect of the lawyer's crude language, sarcasm and casual attitude on the tone and quality of the counseling session? What does the lawyer convey to the client when the lawyer refers to his claim as "this little enterprise"? In what ways does the lawyer's behavior fail to meet the legal profession's standards of conduct and values? What effect may the lawyer's conduct have on the client's perception of lawyers and the legal profession?

2:40: How well does the lawyer explain the relevant law to the client? Does the lawyer's description of prior cases explain how the law will apply to the client's situation? What does the lawyer's explanation of the law say about how seriously he takes his professional obligations and the client's situation? The lawyer resists the client's efforts to distinguish his situation from the cases cited by the lawyer. What are the risks of dismissing a client's input?

4:41: The lawyer expresses his opinion that the client is involved in a scheme to extract gifts from wealthy patients. Has the lawyer done sufficient factual investigation to reach that conclusion? Do the client's statements or conduct support that conclusion? What techniques can a lawyer use to inquire into the client's credibility and motivations without undermining rapport, communication and the lawyer-client relationship?

The lawyer makes assumptions about the client's character and integrity. Why might the lawyer assume the worst of this client? What is the impact of these assumptions on the lawyer-client relationship and the quality of the counseling?

As the meeting becomes more heated, the client yells, "I'm paying you the money. Do what I tell you!" The lawyer responds that he is not a "public bus" required to pick up anyone seeking a ride. What does this exchange reveal about the lawyer's and client's views of their roles in the lawyer-client relationship? How do these views comport with the allocation of authority between lawyer and client set out in Rule 1.2 of the ABA Model Rules of Professional Responsibility?

6:10: The lawyer and client discuss the conditions under which the lawyer will agree to take on the client's case. Does the lawyer's conduct comport with professional and ethical standards? What are the implications of the lawyer asking for "a premium" to proceed with a difficult case? What about when the lawyer threatens to get "amnesia" about the case if the client doesn't make a decision quickly? Even if the lawyer is paid "win, lose or draw," is it accurate to say that he has "no skin in the game"? In what ways do lawyers have a stake in the outcome of their client's matters?

FOR FURTHER DISCUSSION

1. If you were the client, how would you feel about this conversation? your choice of lawyer? the legal profession?

2. Does the lawyer present options to the client and counsel him about their risks and benefits? Does he facilitate client decision-making? Despite his tone, language and attitude, does the lawyer offer the client any sound legal advice or counseling?

3. If, after a thorough investigation, a lawyer believes that their client stands no chance at prevailing on their claim, what is an effective way of communicating that to the client? What are the lawyer's options in addressing the client's situation?

4. What techniques can a lawyer use to deescalate a heated discussion with a client?

5. What would you do if you were present at or overheard this conversation between a lawyer in your office and a client?

6. To what extent might the similarities in race, gender and age between the lawyer and client affect the tone and conduct of the meeting? Might the lawyer project his own biases and attitudes on a client who looks like him and assume that they would find a sympathetic audience? Would the client be more likely to tolerate the lawyer's behavior because the two share many attributes? Conversely, would the meeting go differently if the lawyer and client were not so similar? if one were younger, not male and/or a person of color?

ANNOTATED TRANSCRIPT

This annotated transcript is designed to be read as you watch the corresponding video. The annotations pose questions about the use, purpose and effect of various lawyering techniques; suggest issues for reflection; and highlight comparisons and contrasts among the different lawyering approaches featured in the videos.

Lawyer: So doc, I called Hearn and he told me to, uh, engage in a, uh, anatomically impossible sex act, if you get what I'm saying.

Snow: He was polite, in other words.

Lawyer: Well, looks like we either gotta, um, walk away from this little enterprise or we gotta, you know, go to battle.

Snow: What do you make the chances of battling?

Lawyer: Eh, you know, there's some ways that we can, some ways that we can, uh, we can maybe make a, make a case out of this.

10.1 Consider how the similarities between the lawyer and client—both are older white men—may contribute to the casual—and often profane—tone of the meeting. How might the tone of this meeting change if a third person—the lawyer's associate, assistant or a law student—were present? Might the lawyer act differently if the client were younger, not male and/or a person of color?

Snow: "Make a case," what do you mean?

Lawyer: Well, you know, they gotta prove up that this will's no good.

Snow: Right. So how do they do that?

Lawyer: Eh, they bring in some witnesses, say she's out of her f****** mind, who'd, uh, who'd give you a, a bridal store or beauty salon or whatever it is. They try to make it out like you took advantage of her or something like that.

Snow: Yeah? Do you think I took advantage of her? Is that what it looks like?

Lawyer: Oh, well, you know, my opinion and a quarter will get you a cup of coffee my friend, you know.

Snow: Yeah, well. I mean, the reason I come to a lawyer is because I want to be steered.

10.2 Does counseling involve "steering"? How should the lawyer guide a client through the decision-making process? What if a client wants to be steered? How can the lawyer do so consistent with client-centered principles?

Lawyer: Well, I mean I can give you, I can give you the chapter and verse of this thing, uh.

Snow: Yeah, go ahead!

Lawyer: Well there's a whole bunch of cases: Tyler v. Tyler, which is, uh, from 2014 so it's kind of a good case. There was some case law having to do with this, uh, something called undu—"undue influence." As to whether, uh, yeah, I'll tell you what happened. Uh, she marries this really rich guy and this is the honest-to-God's truth, she discovers on their wedding night that he has changed his will to cut her out and, uh, well, things go downhill from there.

Snow: I would imagine.

Lawyer: Yeah, no s***. And then she—and then he dies and she challenges the will, saying, uh, saying that, uh, the daughter and son inveigled him to change his will before he put the ring on her finger.

Snow: Mm-hmm.

Lawyer: Which probably was true. So, you know. Eh, you know, you can see where this is gonna go. They're gonna say you put the magnet hat on her and the next thing you know she's giving you, uh, the beauty store.

10.3 How effectively does the lawyer explain the law that governs the client's claim? Does the client have the information necessary to understand the lawyer's conclusion that his legal claim is weak?

Snow: But I didn't marry her! I didn't marry her.

Lawyer: Well, I mean, you know. . .I don't know what you did, my friend.

Snow: I didn't do anything to her! All I did was—

Lawyer: Yeah, you cured her of opioid addiction for, what, two—how long was she cured before she died?

Snow: She died suddenly. It's—I don't know, it's a couple of months.

Lawyer: You give a guarantee with this thing?

Snow: Come on, a guarantee? No! No, it's an experiment. I don't make any bones about that.

Lawyer: You cured her for two weeks, then she dies and you get the beauty store.

Snow: Hey! But, but you're implying that I had some kind of improper relationship with this woman and that's just so not true and unfair and that's what her, her stupid—

Lawyer: How about I do this? I'm not gonna "imply." I am going to tell you what I think is going on here.

Snow: Right, you go ahead and tell me.

Lawyer: I think you get this rich old broad in, you f*** around with her, uh, you convince her that your magnet hat is gonna cure her disease and, uh, cancer or whatever else. Then she f****** dies and you're taking her and her family to the cleaners, is what I think. No? Well, I mean—

Snow: That is just so un—that's really over the top! I mean the, the—I, I put my life into this, into developing this treatment. Can I help it if it works? Can I help it if she likes it?

Lawyer: Well we don't know it works, ya know.

Snow: Well, she thought it worked!

Lawyer: I'm just telling you, as a man on the street, you look at this thing. . .

Snow: It's—but it's not about the men in the street, this is about—

Lawyer: Well I mean, Jesus, assume I'm the judge. I mean, what the f***?

Snow: No! She used this and, and sh—and it worked for her. She was grateful—

Lawyer: Oh, for two weeks! Right?

10.4 The lawyer attacks the client's motivations and the legitimacy of his addiction therapy, telling the client that these derogatory accusations are "what I think is going on here." What are the risks of testing the client's story in this way? Compare the lawyer's approach here with how the lawyers in Snow Counseling 1 and 2 counsel their clients about potential weaknesses in the case. See notes 8.3 and 9.4. What are more effective ways to investigate weaknesses in the client's case without alienating the client and undermining the lawyer-client relationship?

Snow: Well, I didn't make any guarantee that it was going to work! But in the interim—

Lawyer: Well Jesus Christ, she could have gotten a cold and gotten the same benefit!

Snow: Come on! Between the time that, that, that she changed her will and the time she died—I mean, no, that's not right. Between the time that we ended the treatment—

Lawyer: Yeah, yeah, the story is, the story is getting a little fluid here—

Snow: Oh, come on! Listen, I'm paying you the money. Do what I tell ya!

Lawyer: Well, ya know I don't have to—I'm not a f****** public bus. I don't have to take everybody who gets on, stands on the corner and waves their hands. I get to choose.

 10.5 What does this heated exchange reveal about the lawyer's and client's views of their roles in the lawyer-client relationship? How do their views comport with the allocation of authority between lawyer and client set out in Rule 1.2 of the ABA Model Rules of Professional Responsibility?

Snow: Of course you don't. But you don't have to sit here and insult me. If you don't want the case, tell me.

Lawyer: Well, ya know, I've got standards, ya know. There's some cases even I won't take.

Snow: Oh yeah? What?

Lawyer: Yeah, well this one might be one of them.

Snow: Okay, well then if that—you don't want it, that's fine. Remember, I got plenty of money. You're the one who says you like the money.

Lawyer: Well, I know, I know, that is a, that is a consideration. . .

Snow: A big consideration! Is there any other consideration?

Lawyer: Well, I don't know, you know. The problem is you on this high horse, you're gonna waltz in there and the f****** judge is gonna say, "who is this guy?"

Snow: Well, who is the judge?

Lawyer: With his magnet hat—

Snow: The magnet ha—well you—

Lawyer: It's a probate judge. Some political hack in the probate district, ya know. What, did I make the law?

Snow: I'm just overwhelmed with your attitude towards the whole thing from beginning to end. If you don't want it—

Lawyer: You know, you're not paying me to sugar-coat this thing.

Snow: —I'll take my business elsewhere.

Lawyer: Alright, well if you wanna go elsewhere, go elsewhere.

Snow: If you're not interested in it, I—

Lawyer: Well, I'm interested in it. I might have to have my—I might have to put a little premium on there here to, to make it worth my. . .

Snow: Alright, well if that's the way it is.

Lawyer: You wanna, you wanna go hell-bent for leather? The girl'll send you another letter and you send me some more money.

Snow: I will think about it.

Lawyer: Well, don't think too long. I could, you know, I get amnesia. I could get something else, you know, some, some better case comes through the door. . .

 10.6 The lawyer's comments about his financial motivations reflect a negative stereotype about the culture and values of the legal profession. This is a familiar trope in the media and popular culture. What is your reaction to this portrayal of the greedy, ethically challenged lawyer?

Snow: You're not, you're not enthusiastic about this case or about my chances, basically.

Lawyer: Well, you know, I get paid win, lose, or draw, my friend.

Snow: Not a contingency fee case then, you're not interested in that.

Lawyer: No, not this case.

Snow: Not this case.

Lawyer: Not this case. No, I ha—I want no skin in the game.

Snow: Alright, so how would you rate the chances, if I go forward, of winning or losing? Fifty-fifty? Forty-sixty? Twenty-eighty?

Lawyer: Well, ya know, it's hard to—

Snow: Five-ninety-five?

Lawyer: It's impossible, because a case like this, it has to do with how good a witness you make, who her—what's it, her son?

Snow: Her son.

Lawyer: Her son comes in, does he look like some kind of grasping, you know, guy or is he really somebody that the judge will like? This case is decided by a judge, not a jury. So, um, or they bring in some witnesses, you know, her, uh, her priest, her rabbi, her imam, uh, you know. She was daffy, you know. I don't know how the f*** it's gonna go. I, I start asking questions and we see where it goes.

Snow: Well, I got the money, I want to see where it goes a little bit further. I'm not happy just walking away from it now.

Lawyer: Rock and roll.

Snow: Let's see—rock and roll, yeah.

Lawyer: Rock and roll, my friend. Alright.

Snow: I mean, you know, the integrity of my invention is at stake and if I just walk away from it—

Lawyer: Oh, you know, I won't give you much advice. The advice I'm gonna give you—let's not bring the magnet hat into this thing, okay? This is all about her and whether or not she could give you her beauty store or bridal store. We're not gonna make this case about the magnet hat.

Snow: Okay.

Lawyer: The only advice I'm gonna give you. Don't tell anybody this business you've got going here. Alright?

10.7 The client premises his decision to pursue the bequest on the grounds that "the integrity of my invention is at stake." Does the lawyer's advice that the client not bring the therapy into the case mesh with the client's goals? Is a strategy not to mention the Khoo Yaa Daa therapy likely to be successful given the relevance of the circumstances under which Ms. Hearn made the contested bequest?

Snow: So be it.

Lawyer: Alright. I'll let you know when we got some action going here.

Snow: Okay.

The End

CREDITS

CLIENT CONVERSATIONS: A SIMULATION AND VIDEO LEARNING GUIDE TO INTERVIEWING AND COUNSELING

Jessica Rubin, Clinical Professor of Law,
Director of Legal Practice

Jennifer Mailly, Clinical Professor of Law,
Associate Dean for Experiential Education

Video Creators

Lucas Lalonde '21

Justin Bell '21

Discussion Materials

Jeffrey Beck '22

Danielle Palmieri '22

Video Attorneys

Valeria Caldwell-Gaines '91

Mark Dubois '77

Erik Lohr '02

Jennifer Mailly

Keisha Palmer '09

Scott Simpson '09

Karla Turekian '96

Regina Wexler '87

Video Clients

Matthew Bader

Alexandra Brokowski

Allan Church

Louanne Cooley '20

Patrick Kania '21

Adam Mackie

Kimberley Parsons

Jonathan Sykes '20

Quyen Truong '20

Technology and Support Services

Johanna Fernandez

Michael Lenn

Abigail Mailly

Charlotte Mailly

Ricardo Mardales

Jared Mikulski

Production and Promotion

Jeanne LeBlanc

AJ Wyman